2009 Supplement

Constitutional Law

ASPEN PUBLISHERS

2009 Supplement

Constitutional Law

Sixth Edition

Geoffrey R. Stone
Harry Kalven, Jr., Distinguished Service Professor of Law
University of Chicago Law School

Louis Michael Seidman
Carmack Waterhouse Professor of Constitutional Law
Georgetown University Law Center

Cass R. Sunstein
Felix Frankfurter Professor of Law
Harvard Law School

Mark V. Tushnet
William Nelson Cromwell Professor of Law
Harvard Law School

Pamela S. Karlan
Kenneth & Harle Montgomery Professor of Public Interest Law
Stanford Law School

Wolters Kluwer
Law & Business

AUSTIN BOSTON CHICAGO NEW YORK THE NETHERLANDS

Aspen Publishers
Attn: Permissions Department
76 Ninth Avenue, 7th Floor
New York, NY 10011-5201

To contact Customer Care, e-mail customer.care@aspenpublishers.com, call 1-800-234-1660, fax 1-800-901-9075, or mail correspondence to:

Aspen Publishers
Attn: Order Department
PO Box 990
Frederick, MD 21705

Printed in the United States of America.

1 2 3 4 5 6 7 8 9 0

ISBN 978-0-7355-7989-7

Library of Congress Cataloging-in-Publication Data

Constitutional law / Geoffrey R. Stone . . . [et al.] — 6th ed.
p. cm.
Includes index.
ISBN 978-0-7355-7719-0 (case bound)
978-0-7355-7989-7 (supplement)
1. Constitutional law — United States. I. Stone, Geoffrey R.

KF4549.C647 2205
342.73 — dc22 2005000567

About Wolters Kluwer Law & Business

Wolters Kluwer Law & Business is a leading provider of research information and workflow solutions in key specialty areas. The strengths of the individual brands of Aspen Publishers, CCH, Kluwer Law International and Loislaw are aligned within Wolters Kluwer Law & Business to provide comprehensive, in-depth solutions and expert-authored content for the legal, professional and education markets.

CCH was founded in 1913 and has served more than four generations of business professionals and their clients. The CCH products in the Wolters Kluwer Law & Business group are highly regarded electronic and print resources for legal, securities, antitrust and trade regulation, government contracting, banking, pension, payroll, employment and labor, and healthcare reimbursement and compliance professionals.

Aspen Publishers is a leading information provider for attorneys, business professionals and law students. Written by preeminent authorities, Aspen products offer analytical and practical information in a range of specialty practice areas from securities law and intellectual property to mergers and acquisitions and pension/benefits. Aspen's trusted legal education resources provide professors and students with high-quality, up-to-date and effective resources for successful instruction and study in all areas of the law.

Kluwer Law International supplies the global business community with comprehensive English-language international legal information. Legal practitioners, corporate counsel and business executives around the world rely on the Kluwer Law International journals, loose-leafs, books and electronic products for authoritative information in many areas of international legal practice.

Loislaw is a premier provider of digitized legal content to small law firm practitioners of various specializations. Loislaw provides attorneys with the ability to quickly and efficiently find the necessary legal information they need, when and where they need it, by facilitating access to primary law as well as state-specific law, records, forms and treatises.

Wolters Kluwer Law & Business, a unit of Wolters Kluwer, is headquartered in New York and Riverwoods, Illinois. Wolters Kluwer is a leading multinational publisher and information services company.

Contents

Table of Cases *ix*
Table of Authorities *xi*

CHAPTER 1. THE ROLE OF THE SUPREME COURT IN THE CONSTITUTIONAL ORDER **1**

District of Columbia v. Heller 1
F. "Case or Controversy" Requirements and the Passive Virtues 38

CHAPTER 2. FEDERALISM AT WORK: CONGRESS AND THE NATIONAL ECONOMY **43**

A. The Values of Federalism and Some Techniques for Implementing Them 43
D. State Regulation of Interstate Commerce 44

CHAPTER 3. THE SCOPE OF CONGRESS'S POWERS: TAXING AND SPENDING, WAR POWERS, INDIVIDUAL RIGHTS, AND STATE AUTONOMY **47**

A. Regulation through Taxing, Spending, and the War Power 47
C. The Tenth Amendment as a Federalism-Based Limitation on Congressional Power 48

CHAPTER 4. THE DISTRIBUTION OF NATIONAL POWERS **51**

A. Introduction 51
B. A Case Study: Presidential Seizure 51
C. Foreign Affairs 52

CHAPTER 5. EQUALITY AND THE CONSTITUTION **53**

C. Equal Protection Methodology: Heightened Scrutiny and the Problem of Race 53
E. Equal Protection Methodology: The Problem of Sexual Orientation 54

CHAPTER 6. IMPLIED FUNDAMENTAL RIGHTS **57**

A. Introduction 57
G. Procedural Due Process 58

CHAPTER 7. FREEDOM OF EXPRESSION **63**

B. Content-Based Restrictions: Dangerous Ideas and Information 63
D. Content-Based Restrictions: "Low" Value Speech 66
E. Content-Neutral Restrictions 67
Pleasant Grove City, Utah v. Summum 70
F. Freedom of the Press 73

CHAPTER 8. THE CONSTITUTION AND RELIGION **75**

B. The Establishment Clause 75
D. Permissible Accommodation 75

Table of Cases

Italics indicate principal and intermediate cases.
All references are to page numbers in the main text.

District of Columbia v. Heller, 78
Caperton v. A.T. Massey Coal Co., 140, 960
District Attorney's Office for the Third Judicial District v. Osborne, 951
FCC v. Fox Television Stations, 1214, 1426
Harper v. Canada, 1357
Haywood v. Drown, 349
Pleasant Grove City, Utah v. Summum, 1317, 1488
Ricci v. DeStefano, 619
Strauss v. Horton 682
Summers v. Earth Island Institute, 117
Varnum v. Brien, 678
Ysursa v. Pocatello Education Association, 1299
Zana v. Turkey, 1066

Table of Authorities

Ammori, Beyond Content-Neutrality: Understanding Content-Based Promotion of Democratic Speech, 61 Fed. Comm. L. J. 273 (2009), 1291

Bezanson, Art and the Constitution 93 Iowa L. Rev. 1593 (2008), 1175

Clark, Separation of Powers as a Safeguard of Federalism, 79 Tex. L. Rev. 1321 (2001), 357

Denning, Reconstructing the Dormant Commerce Clause Doctrine, 50 Wm. & Mary L. Rev. 417 (2008), 238

Erbsen, Horizontal Federalism, 93 Minn. L. Rev. 493 (2008), 234

Feeley, M. and Rubin, E., Federalism: Political Identity and Tragic Compromise (2009), 172

Galle, Federal Grants, State Decisions, 88 B.U.L. Rev. 875 (2008), 297

Gellman & Looper-Friedman, Thou Shalt Use the Equal Protection Clause for Religion Cases (Not Just the Establishment Clause), 10 U. Pa. J. Const'l L. 666 (2008), 1537

Healy, Brandenburg in a Time of Terror, 84 Notre Dame L. Rev. 655 (2009), 1042

Jones, Avalanche or Undue Alarm? An Empirical Study of Subpoenas Received by the New Media, 93 Minn. L. Rev. 585 (2008), 1406

Krotoszynski, The Return of Seditious Libel, 55 UCLA L. Rev. 1239 (2008), 1274

Luban, Lawfare and Legal Ethics in Guantanamo, 60 Stan. L. Rev. 1981 (2008), 392

Norton, The Measure of Government Speech: Identifying Expression's Source, 88 B.U.L. Rev. 587 (2008), 1313
Primus, When Should Original Meaning Matter?, 107 Mich. L. Rev. 165 (2008), 713
Richards, Intellectual Privacy, 87 Tex. L. Rev. 387 (2008), 1067
Siegel, N., Dole's Future: A Strategic Analysis, 16 S. Ct. Econ. Rev. 165 (2008), 295
Symposium, Return to Missouri v. Holland: Federalism and International Law, 73 Mo. L. Rev. 921 (2008), 332
Tushnet, M., *Heller* and the New Originalism, 69 Ohio St. L.J. 609 (2008), 715
Tushnet, M., The Inevitable Globalization of Constitutional Law, 49 Va. J. Int'l L. 985 (2009), 370
Vazquez, Missouri v. Holland's Second Holding, 73 Mo. L. Rev. 939 (2008), 332
Vazquez, The Separation of Powers as a Safeguard of Nationalism, 83 Notre Dame L. Rev. 1601 1606 (2008), 357
Volokh, Symbolic Expression and the Original Meaning of the First Amendment, 97 Geo. L.J. 1057 (2009), 1325
Wells, Privacy and Funeral Protests, 87 N.C. L. Rev. 151 (2008), 1273

1
THE ROLE OF THE SUPREME COURT IN THE CONSTITUTIONAL ORDER

Page 78. Before Section E, add the following:

DISTRICT OF COLUMBIA v. HELLER

554 U.S. ____ (2008)

JUSTICE SCALIA delivered the opinion of the Court.

We consider whether a District of Columbia prohibition on the possession of usable handguns in the home violates the Second Amendment to the Constitution. . . .

II

A

The Second Amendment provides: "A well regulated Militia, being necessary to the security of a free State, the right of the people to keep and bear Arms, shall not be infringed." In interpreting this text, we are guided by the principle that "[t]he Constitution was written to be understood by the voters; its words and phrases were used in their normal and ordinary as distinguished from technical meaning." . . .

The two sides in this case have set out very different interpretations of the Amendment. Petitioners and today's dissenting Justices believe that it protects only the right to possess and carry a firearm in connection with militia service.

Respondent argues that it protects an individual right to possess a firearm unconnected with service in a militia, and to use that arm for traditionally lawful purposes, such as self-defense within the home.

The Second Amendment is naturally divided into two parts: its prefatory clause and its operative clause. The former does not limit the latter grammatically, but rather announces a purpose....

Logic demands that there be a link between the stated purpose and the command. The Second Amendment would be nonsensical if it read, "A well regulated Militia, being necessary to the security of a free State, the right of the people to petition for redress of grievances shall not be infringed." [But a] prefatory clause does not limit or expand the scope of the operative clause. [Therefore,] while we will begin our textual analysis with the operative clause, we will return to the prefatory clause to ensure that our reading of the operative clause is consistent with the announced purpose.

1. Operative Clause.

a. "Right of the People." The first salient feature of the operative clause is that it codifies a "right of the people." The unamended Constitution and the Bill of Rights use the phrase "right of the people" two other times, in the First Amendment's Assembly-and-Petition Clause and in the Fourth Amendment's Search-and-Seizure Clause. The Ninth Amendment uses very similar terminology. [All] three of these instances unambiguously refer to individual rights, not "collective" rights, or rights that may be exercised only through participation in some corporate body....

What is more, in all six other provisions of the Constitution that mention "the people," the term unambiguously refers to all members of the political community, not an unspecified subset....

This contrasts markedly with the phrase "the militia" in the prefatory clause. As we will describe below, the "militia" in colonial America consisted of a subset of "the people"—those who were male, able bodied, and within a certain age range. Reading the Second Amendment as protecting only the right to "keep and bear Arms" in an organized militia therefore fits poorly with the operative clause's description of the holder of that right as "the people."

We start therefore with a strong presumption that the Second Amendment right is exercised individually and belongs to all Americans.

b. "Keep and Bear Arms." We move now from the holder of the right—"the people"—to the substance of the right: "to keep and bear Arms."

Before addressing the verbs "keep" and "bear," we interpret their object: "Arms." The 18th-century meaning is no different from the meaning today. The 1773 edition of Samuel Johnson's dictionary defined "arms" as "weapons of offence, or armour of defence." Timothy Cunningham's important 1771 legal dictionary defined "arms" as "any thing that a man wears for his defence, or takes into his hands, or useth in wrath to cast at or strike another."

The term was applied, then as now, to weapons that were not specifically designed for military use and were not employed in a military capacity. For instance, Cunningham's legal dictionary gave as an example of usage: "Servants and labourers shall use bows and arrows on Sundays, &c. and not bear other arms." [Although] one founding-era thesaurus limited "arms" (as opposed to "weapons") to "instruments of offence *generally* made use of in war," even that source stated that all firearms constituted "arms."

Some have made the argument, bordering on the frivolous, that only those arms in existence in the 18th century are protected by the Second Amendment. We do not interpret constitutional rights that way. Just as the First Amendment protects modern forms of communications, and the Fourth Amendment applies to modern forms of search, the Second Amendment extends, prima facie, to all instruments that constitute bearable arms, even those that were not in existence at the time of the founding.

We turn to the phrases "keep arms" and "bear arms." Johnson defined "keep" as, most relevantly, "[t]o retain; not to lose," and "[t]o have in custody." Webster defined it as "[t]o hold; to retain in one's power or possession." No party has apprised us of an idiomatic meaning of "keep Arms." Thus, the most natural reading of "keep Arms" in the Second Amendment is to "have weapons."

The phrase "keep arms" was not prevalent in the written documents of the founding period that we have found, but there are a few examples, all of which favor viewing the right to "keep Arms" as an individual right unconnected with militia service. William Blackstone, for example, wrote that Catholics convicted of not attending service in the Church of England suffered certain penalties, one of which was that they were not permitted to "keep arms in their houses." ["Keep] arms" was simply a common way of referring to possessing arms, for militiamen *and everyone else*.

At the time of the founding, as now, to "bear" meant to "carry." When used with "arms," however, the term has a meaning that refers to carrying for a particular purpose — confrontation. [Although] the phrase implies that the carrying of the weapon is for the purpose of "offensive or defensive action," it in no way connotes participation in a structured military organization.

From our review of founding-era sources, we conclude that this natural meaning was also the meaning that "bear arms" had in the 18th century. In numerous instances, "bear arms" was unambiguously used to refer to the carrying of weapons outside of an organized militia. The most prominent examples are those most relevant to the Second Amendment: Nine state constitutional provisions written in the 18th century or the first two decades of the 19th, which enshrined a right of citizens to "bear arms in defense of themselves and the state" or "bear arms in defense of himself and the state." It is clear from those formulations that "bear arms" did not refer only to carrying a weapon in an organized military unit. Justice James Wilson interpreted the Pennsylvania Constitution's arms-bearing right, for example, as a recognition of the natural right of defense "of one's person or house" — what he called the law of "self preservation." That was also the interpretation of those state constitutional provisions adopted by pre-Civil War state courts....

The phrase "bear Arms" also had at the time of the founding an idiomatic meaning that was significantly different from its natural meaning: "to serve as a soldier, do military service, fight" or "to wage war." But it *unequivocally* bore that idiomatic meaning only when followed by the preposition "against," which was in turn followed by the target of the hostilities. (That is how, for example, our Declaration of Independence § 28, used the phrase: "He has constrained our fellow Citizens taken Captive on the high Seas to bear Arms against their Country.... ")....

In any event, the meaning of "bear arms" that petitioners and Justice Stevens propose is *not even* the (sometimes) idiomatic meaning. Rather, they manufacture a hybrid definition, whereby "bear arms" connotes the actual carrying of arms (and therefore is not really an idiom) but only in the service of an organized militia. No dictionary has ever adopted that definition, and we have been apprised of no source that indicates that it carried that meaning at the time of the founding. But it is easy to see why petitioners and the dissent are driven to the hybrid definition. Giving "bear Arms" its idiomatic meaning would cause the protected right to consist of the right to be a soldier or to wage war — an absurdity that no commentator has ever endorsed. Worse still, the phrase "keep and bear Arms" would be incoherent. The word "Arms" would have two different meanings at once: "weapons" (as the object of "keep") and (as the object of "bear") one-half of an idiom. It would be rather like saying "He filled and kicked the bucket" to mean "He filled the bucket and died." Grotesque....

Justice Stevens places great weight on James Madison's inclusion of a conscientious-objector clause in his original draft of the Second Amendment: "but no person religiously scrupulous of bearing arms, shall be compelled to render military service in person." He argues that this clause establishes that the drafters of the Second Amendment intended "bear Arms" to refer only to military service. It is always perilous to derive the meaning of an adopted provision from another provision deleted in the drafting process. In any case, what Justice Stevens would conclude from the deleted provision does not follow. It was not meant to exempt from military service those who objected to going to war but had no scruples about personal gunfights. Quakers opposed the use of arms not just for militia service, but for any violent purpose whatsoever — so much so that Quaker frontiersmen were forbidden to use arms to defend their families, even though "[i]n such circumstances the temptation to seize a hunting rifle or knife in self-defense... must sometimes have been almost overwhelming." [Thus], the most natural interpretation of Madison's deleted text is that those opposed to carrying weapons for potential violent confrontation would not be "compelled to render military service," in which such carrying would be required.

Finally, Justice Stevens suggests that "keep and bear Arms" was some sort of term of art, presumably akin to "hue and cry" or "cease and desist." [Justice] Stevens believes that the unitary meaning of "keep and bear Arms" is established by the Second Amendment's calling it a "right" (singular) rather than "rights" (plural). There is nothing to this. State constitutions of the founding period routinely grouped multiple (related) guarantees under a singular "right," and the First Amendment protects the "right [singular] of the people peaceably to assemble, and to petition the Government for a redress of grievances."....

c. Meaning of the Operative Clause. Putting all of these textual elements together, we find that they guarantee the individual right to possess and carry weapons in case of confrontation. This meaning is strongly confirmed by the historical background of the Second Amendment. We look to this because it has always been widely understood that the Second Amendment, like the First and Fourth Amendments, codified a *pre-existing* right. The very text of the Second Amendment implicitly recognizes the pre-existence of the right and declares only that it "shall not be infringed." As we said in *United States v. Cruikshank*, 92 U.S. 542, 553 (1876), "[t]his is not a right granted by the Constitution. Neither is it in any manner dependent upon that instrument for its existence. The Second amendment declares that it shall not be infringed...."

Between the Restoration and the Glorious Revolution, the Stuart Kings Charles II and James II succeeded in using select militias loyal to them to suppress political dissidents, in part by disarming their opponents. [These] experiences caused Englishmen to be extremely wary of concentrated military forces run by the state and to be jealous of their arms. They accordingly obtained an assurance from William and Mary, in the Declaration of Right (which was codified as the English Bill of Rights), that Protestants would never be disarmed: "That the subjects which are Protestants may have arms for their defense suitable to their conditions and as allowed by law." This right has long been understood to be the predecessor to our Second Amendment. It was clearly an individual right, having nothing whatever to do with service in a militia. To be sure, it was an individual right not available to the whole population, given that it was restricted to Protestants, and like all written English rights it was held only against the Crown, not Parliament. But it was secured to them as individuals, according to "libertarian political principles," not as members of a fighting force.

By the time of the founding, the right to have arms had become fundamental for English subjects. Blackstone, whose works, we have said, "constituted the preeminent authority on English law for the founding generation," cited the arms provision of the Bill of Rights as one of the fundamental rights of Englishmen. [It] was, he said, "the natural right of resistance and self-preservation," and "the right of having and using arms for self-preservation and defence." Thus, the right secured in 1689 as a result of the Stuarts' abuses was by the time of the founding understood to be an individual right protecting against both public and private violence.

And, of course, what the Stuarts had tried to do to their political enemies, George III had tried to do to the colonists. In the tumultuous decades of the 1760's and 1770's, the Crown began to disarm the inhabitants of the most rebellious areas. [The colonists] understood the right to enable individuals to defend themselves. As the most important early American edition of Blackstone's Commentaries (by the law professor and former Antifederalist St. George Tucker) made clear in the notes to the description of the arms right, Americans understood the "right of self-preservation" as permitting a citizen to "repe[l] force by force" when "the intervention of society in his behalf, may be too late to prevent an injury."

There seems to us no doubt, on the basis of both text and history, that the Second Amendment conferred an individual right to keep and bear arms. Of course the right was not unlimited, just as the First Amendment's right of free speech was not. Thus, we do not read the Second Amendment to protect the right of citizens to carry arms for *any sort* of confrontation, just as we do not read the First Amendment to protect the right of citizens to speak for *any purpose*. Before turning to limitations upon the individual right, however, we must determine whether the prefatory clause of the Second Amendment comports with our interpretation of the operative clause.

2. Prefatory Clause.

The prefatory clause reads: "A well regulated Militia, being necessary to the security of a free State.... "

a. "Well-Regulated Militia." In *United States v. Miller*, 307 U.S. 174, 179 (1939), we explained that "the Militia comprised all males physically capable of acting in concert for the common defense." That definition comports with founding-era sources.

Petitioners take a seemingly narrower view of the militia, stating that "[m]ilitias are the state- and congressionally-regulated military forces described in the Militia Clauses (art. I, § 8, cls. 15-16)." [We] believe that petitioners identify the wrong thing, namely, the organized militia. Unlike armies and navies, which Congress is given the power to create ("to raise... Armies"; "to provide... a Navy," Art. I, § 8, cls. 12-13), the militia is assumed by Article

I already to be *in existence.* [and to consist of] all able-bodied men. [Although] the militia consists of all able-bodied men, the federally organized militia may consist of a subset of them.

Finally, the adjective "well-regulated" implies nothing more than the imposition of proper discipline and training.

b. "Security of a Free State."...

There are many reasons why the militia was thought to be "necessary to the security of a free state." First, of course, it is useful in repelling invasions and suppressing insurrections. Second, it renders large standing armies unnecessary. [Third,] when the able-bodied men of a nation are trained in arms and organized, they are better able to resist tyranny.

3. Relationship between Prefatory Clause and Operative Clause

We reach the question, then: Does the preface fit with an operative clause that creates an individual right to keep and bear arms? It fits perfectly, once one knows the history that the founding generation knew and that we have described above. That history showed that the way tyrants had eliminated a militia consisting of all the able-bodied men was not by banning the militia but simply by taking away the people's arms, enabling a select militia or standing army to suppress political opponents. This is what had occurred in England that prompted codification of the right to have arms in the English Bill of Rights.

[During] the 1788 ratification debates, the fear that the federal government would disarm the people in order to impose rule through a standing army or select militia was pervasive in Antifederalist rhetoric....

It is therefore entirely sensible that the Second Amendment's prefatory clause announces the purpose for which the right was codified: to prevent elimination of the militia. The prefatory clause does not suggest that preserving the militia was the only reason Americans valued the ancient right; most undoubtedly thought it even more important for self-defense and hunting. But the threat that the new Federal Government would destroy the citizens' militia by taking away their arms was the reason that right—unlike some other English rights—was codified in a written Constitution....

B

Our interpretation is confirmed by analogous arms-bearing rights in state constitutions that preceded and immediately followed adoption of the Second Amendment....

Between 1789 and 1820, nine States adopted Second Amendment analogues. Four of them [referred] to the right of the people to "bear arms in defence of themselves and the State." Another three States [used] the even more individualistic phrasing that each citizen has the "right to bear arms in defence of himself and the State." Finally, two States [used] "common defence" language....

D

We now address how the Second Amendment was interpreted from immediately after its ratification through the end of the 19th century. Before proceeding, however, we take issue with Justice Stevens' equating of these sources with postenactment legislative history, a comparison that betrays a fundamental misunderstanding of a court's interpretive task. [That phrase] most certainly does not refer to the examination of a variety of legal and other sources to determine *the public understanding* of a legal text in the period after its enactment or ratification. That sort of inquiry is a critical tool of constitutional interpretation. As we will show, virtually all interpreters of the Second Amendment in the century after its enactment interpreted the amendment as we do.

1. Post-ratification Commentary

Three important founding-era legal scholars interpreted the Second Amendment in published writings. All three understood it to protect an individual right unconnected with militia service....

2. Pre-Civil War Case Law

The 19th-century cases that interpreted the Second Amendment universally support an individual right unconnected to militia service....

Many early 19th-century state cases indicated that the Second Amendment right to bear arms was an individual right unconnected to militia service, though subject to certain restrictions. A Virginia case in 1824 holding that the Constitution did not extend to free blacks explained that "numerous restrictions imposed on [blacks] in our Statute Book, many of which are inconsistent with the letter and spirit of the Constitution, both of this State and of the United States as respects the free whites, demonstrate, that, here, those instruments have not been considered to extend equally to both classes of our population. We will only instance the restriction upon the migration of free blacks into this State, and upon their right to bear arms." *Aldridge v. Commonwealth*, 4 Va. 447 (Gen. Ct.). [An] 1829 decision by the Supreme Court of Michigan said: "The constitution of the United States also grants to the citizen the right to keep and bear arms. But the grant of this privilege cannot be construed into the right in him who keeps a gun to destroy his neighbor. No rights are intended to be granted by the constitution for an unlawful or unjustifiable purpose."

In *Nunn v. State*, 1 Ga. 243, 251 (1846), the Georgia Supreme Court construed the Second Amendment as protecting the "*natural* right of self-defence" and therefore struck down a ban on carrying pistols openly....

Likewise, in *State v. Chandler*, 5 La. Ann. 489, 490 (1850), the Louisiana Supreme Court held that citizens had a right to carry arms openly: "This is the right guaranteed by the Constitution of the United States, and which is calculated to incite men to a manly and noble defence of themselves, if necessary, and of their country, without any tendency to secret advantages and unmanly assassinations." . . .

3. Post-Civil War Legislation

In the aftermath of the Civil War, there was an outpouring of discussion of the Second Amendment in Congress and in public discourse, as people debated whether and how to secure constitutional rights for newly free slaves. Since those discussions took place 75 years after the ratification of the Second Amendment, they do not provide as much insight into its original meaning as earlier sources. Yet those born and educated in the early 19th century faced a widespread effort to limit arms ownership by a large number of citizens; their understanding of the origins and continuing significance of the Amendment is instructive.

Blacks were routinely disarmed by Southern States after the Civil War. Those who opposed these injustices frequently stated that they infringed blacks' constitutional right to keep and bear arms. Needless to say, the claim was not that blacks were being prohibited from carrying arms in an organized state militia. [A] joint congressional Report decried:

> in some parts of [South Carolina], armed parties are, without proper authority, engaged in seizing all fire-arms found in the hands of the freemen. Such conduct is in clear and direct violation of their personal rights as guaranteed by the Constitution of the United States, which declares that "the right of the people to keep and bear arms shall not be infringed." The freedmen of South Carolina have shown by their peaceful and orderly conduct that they can safely be trusted with fire-arms, and they need them to kill game for subsistence, and to protect their crops from destruction by birds and animals. . . .

Congress enacted the Freedmen's Bureau Act on July 16, 1866. Section 14 stated:

> [T]he right . . . to have full and equal benefit of all laws and proceedings concerning personal liberty, personal security, and the acquisition, enjoyment, and disposition of estate, real and personal, including the constitutional right to bear arms, shall be secured to and enjoyed by all the citizens . . . without respect to race or color, or previous condition of slavery. . . .

The understanding that the Second Amendment gave freed blacks the right to keep and bear arms was reflected in congressional discussion of the bill. . . .

Similar discussion attended the passage of the Civil Rights Act of 1871 and the Fourteenth Amendment. . . .

4. Post-Civil War Commentators.

Every late-19th-century legal scholar that we have read interpreted the Second Amendment to secure an individual right unconnected with militia service. The most famous was the judge and professor Thomas Cooley, who wrote a massively popular 1868 Treatise on Constitutional Limitations. Concerning the Second Amendment it said:

> Among the other defences to personal liberty should be mentioned the right of the people to keep and bear arms.... The alternative to a standing army is "a well-regulated militia," but this cannot exist unless the people are trained to bearing arms. How far it is in the power of the legislature to regulate this right, we shall not undertake to say, as happily there has been very little occasion to discuss that subject by the courts....

E

We now ask whether any of our precedents forecloses the conclusions we have reached about the meaning of the Second Amendment.

United States v. Cruikshank, in the course of vacating the convictions of members of a white mob for depriving blacks of their right to keep and bear arms, held that the Second Amendment does not by its own force apply to anyone other than the Federal Government. [The] limited discussion of the Second Amendment in *Cruikshank* supports, if anything, the individual-rights interpretation. There was no claim in *Cruikshank* that the victims had been deprived of their right to carry arms in a militia; indeed, the Governor had disbanded the local militia unit the year before the mob's attack....

Presser v. Illinois, 116 U.S. 252 (1886), held that the right to keep and bear arms was not violated by a law that forbade "bodies of men to associate together as military organizations, or to drill or parade with arms in cities and towns unless authorized by law." This does not refute the individual-rights interpretation of the Amendment; no one supporting that interpretation has contended that States may not ban such groups....

Justice Stevens places overwhelming reliance upon this Court's decision in *United States v. Miller*, 307 U.S. 174 (1939). "[H]undreds of judges," we are told, "have relied on the view of the amendment we endorsed there," and "[e]ven if the textual and historical arguments on both side of the issue were evenly balanced, respect for the well-settled views of all of our predecessors on this Court, and for the rule of law itself... would prevent most jurists from endorsing such a dramatic upheaval in the law." And what is, according to Justice Stevens, the holding of *Miller* that demands such obeisance? That the Second Amendment "protects the right to keep and bear arms for certain military purposes, but that it does not curtail the legislature's power to regulate the nonmilitary use and ownership of weapons."

Nothing so clearly demonstrates the weakness of Justice Stevens' case. *Miller* did not hold that and cannot possibly be read to have held that. The judgment in the case upheld against a Second Amendment challenge two men's federal convictions for transporting an unregistered short-barreled shotgun in interstate commerce, in violation of the National Firearms Act. It is entirely clear that the Court's basis for saying that the Second Amendment did not apply was *not* that the defendants were "bear[ing] arms" not "for... military purposes" but for "nonmilitary use." Rather, it was that the *type of weapon at issue* was not eligible for Second Amendment protection....

This holding is not only consistent with, but positively suggests, that the Second Amendment confers an individual right to keep and bear arms (though only arms that "have some reasonable relationship to the preservation or efficiency of a well regulated militia"). Had the Court believed that the Second Amendment protects only those serving in the militia, it would have been odd to examine the character of the weapon rather than simply note that the two crooks were not militiamen....

It is particularly wrongheaded to read *Miller* for more than what it said, because the case did not even purport to be a thorough examination of the Second Amendment. Justice Stevens claims that the opinion reached its conclusion "[a]fter reviewing many of the same sources that are discussed at greater length by the Court today." Not many, which was not entirely the Court's fault. The respondent made no appearance in the case, neither filing a brief nor appearing at oral argument; the Court heard from no one but the Government (reason enough, one would think, not to make that case the beginning and the end of this Court's consideration of the Second Amendment). [This] is the mighty rock upon which the dissent rests its case.[1]

We may as well consider at this point (for we will have to consider eventually) *what* types of weapons *Miller* permits. Read in isolation, *Miller*'s phrase "part of ordinary military equipment" could mean that only those weapons useful in warfare are protected. That would be a startling reading of the opinion, since it would mean that the National Firearms Act's restrictions on machineguns (not challenged in *Miller*) might be unconstitutional, machineguns being useful in warfare in 1939. We think that *Miller*'s "ordinary military equipment" language must be read in tandem with what comes after: "[O]rdinarily when

1. As for the "hundreds of judges" who have relied on the view of the Second Amendment Justice Stevens claims we endorsed in *Miller*: If so, they overread *Miller*. And their erroneous reliance upon an uncontested and virtually unreasoned case cannot nullify the reliance of millions of Americans (as our historical analysis has shown) upon the true meaning of the right to keep and bear arms. In any event, it should not be thought that the cases decided by these judges would necessarily have come out differently under a proper interpretation of the right.

called for [militia] service [able-bodied] men were expected to appear bearing arms supplied by themselves and of the kind in common use at the time." The traditional militia was formed from a pool of men bringing arms "in common use at the time" for lawful purposes like self-defense. "In the colonial and revolutionary war era, [small-arms] weapons used by militiamen and weapons used in defense of person and home were one and the same." [We] therefore read *Miller* to say only that the Second Amendment does not protect those weapons not typically possessed by law-abiding citizens for lawful purposes, such as short-barreled shotguns. That accords with the historical understanding of the scope of the right, see Part III, *infra*....

We conclude that nothing in our precedents forecloses our adoption of the original understanding of the Second Amendment. It should be unsurprising that such a significant matter has been for so long judicially unresolved. For most of our history, the Bill of Rights was not thought applicable to the States, and the Federal Government did not significantly regulate the possession of firearms by law-abiding citizens. Other provisions of the Bill of Rights have similarly remained unilluminated for lengthy periods. This Court first held a law to violate the *First Amendment's* guarantee of freedom of speech in 1931, almost 150 years after the Amendment was ratified, see *Near v. Minnesota ex rel. Olson*, 283 U.S. 697 (1931), and it was not until after World War II that we held a law invalid under the Establishment Clause, see *Illinois ex rel. McCollum v. Bd. of Educ.*, 333 U.S. 203 (1948)....

III

Like most rights, the right secured by the Second Amendment is not unlimited. From Blackstone through the 19th-century cases, commentators and courts routinely explained that the right was not a right to keep and carry any weapon whatsoever in any manner whatsoever and for whatever purpose. For example, the majority of the 19th-century courts to consider the question held that prohibitions on carrying concealed weapons were lawful under the Second Amendment or state analogues. Although we do not undertake an exhaustive historical analysis today of the full scope of the Second Amendment, nothing in our opinion should be taken to cast doubt on longstanding prohibitions on the possession of firearms by felons and the mentally ill, or laws forbidding the carrying of firearms in sensitive places such as schools and government buildings, or laws imposing conditions and qualifications on the commercial sale of arms.[26]

---

26. We identify these presumptively lawful regulatory measures only as examples; our list does not purport to be exhaustive.

We also recognize another important limitation on the right to keep and carry arms. *Miller* said, as we have explained, that the sorts of weapons protected were those "in common use at the time." We think that limitation is fairly supported by the historical tradition of prohibiting the carrying of "dangerous and unusual weapons."

It may be objected that if weapons that are most useful in military service — M-16 rifles and the like — may be banned, then the Second Amendment right is completely detached from the prefatory clause. But as we have said, the conception of the militia at the time of the Second Amendment's ratification was the body of all citizens capable of military service, who would bring the sorts of lawful weapons that they possessed at home to militia duty. It may well be true today that a militia, to be as effective as militias in the 18th century, would require sophisticated arms that are highly unusual in society at large. Indeed, it may be true that no amount of small arms could be useful against modern-day bombers and tanks. But the fact that modern developments have limited the degree of fit between the prefatory clause and the protected right cannot change our interpretation of the right.

IV

We turn finally to the law at issue here. As we have said, the law totally bans handgun possession in the home. It also requires that any lawful firearm in the home be disassembled or bound by a trigger lock at all times, rendering it inoperable.

As the quotations earlier in this opinion demonstrate, the inherent right of self-defense has been central to the Second Amendment right. The handgun ban amounts to a prohibition of an entire class of "arms" that is overwhelmingly chosen by American society for that lawful purpose. The prohibition extends, moreover, to the home, where the need for defense of self, family, and property is most acute. Under any of the standards of scrutiny that we have applied to enumerated constitutional rights,[27] banning from the home "the most preferred

27. Justice Breyer correctly notes that this law, like almost all laws, would pass rational-basis scrutiny. But rational-basis scrutiny is a mode of analysis we have used when evaluating laws under constitutional commands that are themselves prohibitions on irrational laws. In those cases, "rational basis" is not just the standard of scrutiny, but the very substance of the constitutional guarantee. Obviously, the same test could not be used to evaluate the extent to which a legislature may regulate a specific, enumerated right, be it the freedom of speech, the guarantee against double jeopardy, the right to counsel, or the right to keep and bear arms. See *United States v. Carolene Products Co.*, 304 U.S. 144, 152, n. 4 (1938) ("There may be narrower scope for operation of the presumption of constitutionality [*i.e.*, narrower than that provided by rational-basis review] when legislation appears

firearm in the nation to 'keep' and use for protection of one's home and family," would fail constitutional muster....

It is no answer to say [that] it is permissible to ban the possession of handguns so long as the possession of other firearms (*i.e.*, long guns) is allowed. It is enough to note, as we have observed, that the American people have considered the handgun to be the quintessential self-defense weapon. There are many reasons that a citizen may prefer a handgun for home defense: It is easier to store in a location that is readily accessible in an emergency; it cannot easily be redirected or wrestled away by an attacker; it is easier to use for those without the upper-body strength to lift and aim a long gun; it can be pointed at a burglar with one hand while the other hand dials the police. Whatever the reason, handguns are the most popular weapon chosen by Americans for self-defense in the home, and a complete prohibition of their use is invalid....

Justice Breyer has devoted most of his separate dissent to the handgun ban. He says that, even assuming the Second Amendment is a personal guarantee of the right to bear arms, the District's prohibition is valid. He first tries to establish this by founding-era historical precedent, pointing to various restrictive laws in the colonial period. [A] 1783 Massachusetts law forbade the residents of Boston to "take into" or "receive into" "any Dwelling House, Stable, Barn, Out-house, Ware-house, Store, Shop or other Building" loaded firearms, and permitted the seizure of any loaded firearms that "shall be found" there. That statute's text and its prologue, which makes clear that the purpose of the prohibition was to eliminate the danger to firefighters posed by the "depositing of loaded Arms" in buildings, give reason to doubt that colonial Boston authorities would have enforced that general prohibition against someone who temporarily loaded a firearm to confront an intruder (despite the law's application in that case). In any case, we would not stake our interpretation of the Second Amendment upon a single law, in effect in a single city, that contradicts the overwhelming weight of other evidence regarding the right to keep and bear arms for defense of the home. The other laws Justice Breyer cites are gunpowder-storage laws that he concedes did not clearly prohibit loaded weapons, but required only that excess gunpowder be kept in a special container or on the top floor of the home. Nothing about those fire-safety laws undermines our analysis; they do not remotely burden the right of self-defense as much as an absolute ban on handguns. Nor, correspondingly, does our analysis suggest the invalidity of laws regulating the storage of firearms to prevent accidents....

---

on its face to be within a specific prohibition of the Constitution, such as those of the first ten amendments . . . "). If all that was required to overcome the right to keep and bear arms was a rational basis, the Second Amendment would be redundant with the separate constitutional prohibitions on irrational laws, and would have no effect.

Justice Breyer moves on to make a broad jurisprudential point: He criticizes us for declining to establish a level of scrutiny for evaluating Second Amendment restrictions. He proposes, explicitly at least, none of the traditionally expressed levels (strict scrutiny, intermediate scrutiny, rational basis), but rather a judge-empowering "interest-balancing inquiry" that "asks whether the statute burdens a protected interest in a way or to an extent that is out of proportion to the statute's salutary effects upon other important governmental interests." After an exhaustive discussion of the arguments for and against gun control, Justice Breyer arrives at his interest-balanced answer: because handgun violence is a problem, because the law is limited to an urban area, and because there were somewhat similar restrictions in the founding period (a false proposition that we have already discussed), the interest-balancing inquiry results in the constitutionality of the handgun ban. QED.

We know of no other enumerated constitutional right whose core protection has been subjected to a freestanding "interest-balancing" approach. The very enumeration of the right takes out of the hands of government — even the Third Branch of Government — the power to decide on a case-by-case basis whether the right is *really worth* insisting upon. A constitutional guarantee subject to future judges' assessments of its usefulness is no constitutional guarantee at all. Constitutional rights are enshrined with the scope they were understood to have when the people adopted them, whether or not future legislatures or (yes) even future judges think that scope too broad. We would not apply an "interest-balancing" approach to the prohibition of a peaceful neo-Nazi march through Skokie. See *National Socialist Party of America v. Skokie*, 432 U.S. 43 (1977) (per curiam). The First Amendment contains the freedom-of-speech guarantee that the people ratified, which included exceptions for obscenity, libel, and disclosure of state secrets, but not for the expression of extremely unpopular and wrong-headed views. The Second Amendment is no different. Like the First, it is the very *product* of an interest-balancing by the people — which Justice Breyer would now conduct for them anew. And whatever else it leaves to future evaluation, it surely elevates above all other interests the right of law-abiding, responsible citizens to use arms in defense of hearth and home.

Justice Breyer chides us for leaving so many applications of the right to keep and bear arms in doubt, and for not providing extensive historical justification for those regulations of the right that we describe as permissible. But since this case represents this Court's first in-depth examination of the Second Amendment, one should not expect it to clarify the entire field, any more than *Reynolds v. United States*, 98 U.S. 145 (1879), our first in-depth Free Exercise Clause case, left that area in a state of utter certainty. And there will be time enough to expound upon the historical justifications for the exceptions we have mentioned if and when those exceptions come before us....

* * *

We are aware of the problem of handgun violence in this country, and we take seriously the concerns raised by the many *amici* who believe that prohibition of handgun ownership is a solution. The Constitution leaves the District of Columbia a variety of tools for combating that problem, including some measures regulating handguns. But the enshrinement of constitutional rights necessarily takes certain policy choices off the table. These include the absolute prohibition of handguns held and used for self-defense in the home. Undoubtedly some think that the Second Amendment is outmoded in a society where our standing army is the pride of our Nation, where well-trained police forces provide personal security, and where gun violence is a serious problem. That is perhaps debatable, but what is not debatable is that it is not the role of this Court to pronounce the Second Amendment extinct....

JUSTICE STEVENS, with whom JUSTICE SOUTER, JUSTICE GINSBURG, and JUSTICE BREYER join, dissenting.

The question presented by this case is not whether the Second Amendment protects a "collective right" or an "individual right." Surely it protects a right that can be enforced by individuals. But a conclusion that the Second Amendment protects an individual right does not tell us anything about the scope of that right.

Guns are used to hunt, for self-defense, to commit crimes, for sporting activities, and to perform military duties. The Second Amendment plainly does not protect the right to use a gun to rob a bank; it is equally clear that it *does* encompass the right to use weapons for certain military purposes. Whether it also protects the right to possess and use guns for nonmilitary purposes like hunting and personal self-defense is the question presented by this case. The text of the Amendment, its history, and our decision in *United States v. Miller*, 307 U.S. 174 (1939), provide a clear answer to that question.

The Second Amendment was adopted to protect the right of the people of each of the several States to maintain a well-regulated militia. It was a response to concerns raised during the ratification of the Constitution that the power of Congress to disarm the state militias and create a national standing army posed an intolerable threat to the sovereignty of the several States. Neither the text of the Amendment nor the arguments advanced by its proponents evidenced the slightest interest in limiting any legislature's authority to regulate private civilian uses of firearms. Specifically, there is no indication that the Framers of the Amendment intended to enshrine the common-law right of self-defense in the Constitution.

In 1934, Congress enacted the National Firearms Act, the first major federal firearms law. Upholding a conviction under that Act, this Court held that, "[i]n the absence of any evidence tending to show that possession or use of a 'shotgun having a barrel of less than eighteen inches in length' at this time has some reasonable relationship to the preservation or efficiency of a well regulated militia, we cannot say that the Second Amendment guarantees the right to keep and bear such an instrument." The view of the Amendment we took in *Miller*— that it protects the right to keep and bear arms for certain military purposes, but that it does not curtail the Legislature's power to regulate the nonmilitary use and ownership of weapons—is both the most natural reading of the Amendment's text and the interpretation most faithful to the history of its adoption.

Since our decision in *Miller,* hundreds of judges have relied on the view of the Amendment we endorsed there; we ourselves affirmed it in 1980. See *Lewis v. United States*, 445 U.S. 55 (1980).[3] No new evidence has surfaced since 1980 supporting the view that the Amendment was intended to curtail the power of Congress to regulate civilian use or misuse of weapons. Indeed, a review of the drafting history of the Amendment demonstrates that its Framers *rejected* proposals that would have broadened its coverage to include such uses.

The opinion the Court announces today fails to identify any new evidence supporting the view that the Amendment was intended to limit the power of Congress to regulate civilian uses of weapons. Unable to point to any such evidence, the Court stakes its holding on a strained and unpersuasive reading of the Amendment's text; significantly different provisions in the 1689 English Bill of Rights, and in various 19th-century State Constitutions; postenactment commentary that was available to the Court when it decided *Miller;* and, ultimately, a feeble attempt to distinguish *Miller* that places more emphasis on the Court's decisional process than on the reasoning in the opinion itself.

Even if the textual and historical arguments on both sides of the issue were evenly balanced, respect for the well-settled views of all of our predecessors on this Court, and for the rule of law itself, would prevent most jurists from endorsing such a dramatic upheaval in the law. As Justice Cardozo observed years ago, the "labor of judges would be increased almost to the breaking point if every past decision could be reopened in every case, and one could not lay one's own course of bricks on the secure foundation of the courses laid by others who had gone before him." The Nature of the Judicial Process 149 (1921)....

I

[T]hree portions of [the Second Amendment's] text merit special focus: the introductory language defining the Amendment's purpose, the class of persons encompassed within its reach, and the unitary nature of the right that it protects.

---

3. Our discussion in *Lewis* was brief but significant. Upholding a conviction for receipt of a firearm by a felon, we wrote: "These legislative restrictions on the use of firearms are neither based upon constitutionally suspect criteria, nor do they entrench upon any constitutionally protected liberties. See *United States v. Miller*. . . ."

"A well regulated Militia, being necessary to the security of a free State"

The preamble to the Second Amendment makes three important points. It identifies the preservation of the militia as the Amendment's purpose; it explains that the militia is necessary to the security of a free State; and it recognizes that the militia must be "well regulated."....

[The] Second Amendment's omission of any statement of purpose related to the right to use firearms for hunting or personal self-defense, is especially striking in light of the fact that the Declarations of Rights of Pennsylvania and Vermont did expressly protect such civilian uses at the time. [The] contrast between those two declarations and the Second Amendment reinforces the clear statement of purpose announced in the Amendment's preamble. It confirms that the Framers' single-minded focus in crafting the constitutional guarantee "to keep and bear arms" was on military uses of firearms, which they viewed in the context of service in state militias....

The Court today tries to denigrate the importance of this clause of the Amendment by beginning its analysis with the Amendment's operative provision and returning to the preamble merely "to ensure that our reading of the operative clause is consistent with the announced purpose." That is not how this Court ordinarily reads such texts, and it is not how the preamble would have been viewed at the time the Amendment was adopted....

"The right of the people"

The centerpiece of the Court's textual argument is its insistence that the words "the people" as used in the Second Amendment must have the same meaning, and protect the same class of individuals, as when they are used in the First and Fourth Amendments. [But] the Court *itself* reads the Second Amendment to protect a "subset" significantly narrower than the class of persons protected by the First and Fourth Amendments; when it finally drills down on the substantive meaning of the Second Amendment, the Court limits the protected class to "law-abiding, responsible citizens." But the class of persons protected by the First and Fourth Amendments is *not* so limited; for even felons (and presumably irresponsible citizens as well) may invoke the protections of those constitutional provisions. The Court offers no way to harmonize its conflicting pronouncements.

The Court also overlooks the significance of the way the Framers used the phrase "the people" in these constitutional provisions. In the First Amendment, [it] is only the right peaceably to assemble, and to petition the Government for a redress of grievances, that is described as a right of "the people." These rights contemplate collective action. While the right peaceably to assemble protects the individual rights of those persons participating in the assembly, its concern is with action engaged in by members of a group, rather than any single individual.

Likewise, although the act of petitioning the Government is a right that can be exercised by individuals, it is primarily collective in nature....

Similarly, the words "the people" in the Second Amendment refer back to the object announced in the Amendment's preamble. They remind us that it is the collective action of individuals having a duty to serve in the militia that the text directly protects and, perhaps more importantly, that the ultimate purpose of the Amendment was to protect the States' share of the divided sovereignty created by the Constitution.

[I]t is true that the Fourth Amendment describes a right that need not be exercised in any collective sense. But that observation does not settle the meaning of the phrase "the people" when used in the Second Amendment. For, as we have seen, the phrase means something quite different in the Petition and Assembly Clauses of the First Amendment....

"To keep and bear Arms"

Although the Court's discussion of these words treats them as two "phrases"—as if they read "to keep" and "to bear"—they describe a unitary right: to possess arms if needed for military purposes and to use them in conjunction with military activities....

The term "bear arms" is a familiar idiom; when used unadorned by any additional words, its meaning is "to serve as a soldier, do military service, fight." One 18th-century dictionary defined "arms" as "weapons of offence, or armour of defence," and another contemporaneous source explained that "[b]y *arms*, we understand those instruments of offence generally made use of in war; such as firearms, swords, & c. By *weapons,* we more particularly mean instruments of other kinds (exclusive of fire-arms), made use of as offensive, on special occasions." Had the Framers wished to expand the meaning of the phrase "bear arms" to encompass civilian possession and use, they could have done so by the addition of phrases such as "for the defense of themselves," as was done in the Pennsylvania and Vermont Declarations of Rights. The *unmodified* use of "bear arms," by contrast, refers most naturally to a military purpose, as evidenced by its use in literally dozens of contemporary texts....

The Amendment's use of the term "keep" in no way contradicts the military meaning conveyed by the phrase "bear arms" and the Amendment's preamble. To the contrary, a number of state militia laws in effect at the time of the Second Amendment's drafting used the term "keep" to describe the requirement that militia members store their arms at their homes, ready to be used for service when necessary....

This reading is confirmed by the fact that the clause protects only one right, rather than two. [The] single right that it does describe is both a duty and a right to have arms available and ready for military service, and to use them for military purposes when necessary.[13] Different language surely would have been used to protect nonmilitary use and possession of weapons from regulation if such an intent had played any role in the drafting of the Amendment....

II

The proper allocation of military power in the new Nation was an issue of central concern for the Framers. The compromises they ultimately reached, reflected in Article I's Militia Clauses and the Second Amendment, represent quintessential examples of the Framers' "splitting the atom of sovereignty."

Two themes relevant to our current interpretive task ran through the debates on the original Constitution. "On the one hand, there was a widespread fear that a national standing Army posed an intolerable threat to individual liberty and to the sovereignty of the separate States." [On] the other hand, the Framers recognized the dangers inherent in relying on inadequately trained militia members "as the primary means of providing for the common defense"; during the Revolutionary War, "[t]his force, though armed, was largely untrained, and its deficiencies were the subject of bitter complaint." In order to respond to those twin concerns, a compromise was reached: Congress would be authorized to raise and support a national Army and Navy, and also to organize, arm, discipline, and provide for the calling forth of "the Militia." U.S. Const., Art. I, § 8, cls. 12-16. The President, at the same time, was empowered as the "Commander in Chief of the Army and Navy of the United States, and of the Militia of the several States, when called into the actual Service of the United States." Art. II, § 2. But, with respect to the militia, a significant reservation was made to the States: Although Congress would have the power to call forth, organize, arm, and discipline the militia, as well as to govern "such Part of them as may be employed in the Service of the United States," the States respectively would retain the right to appoint the officers and to train the militia in accordance with the discipline prescribed by Congress. Art. I, § 8, cl. 16.

But the original Constitution's retention of the militia and its creation of divided authority over that body did not prove sufficient to allay fears about the dangers posed by a standing army. For it was perceived by some that Article I contained a significant gap: While it empowered Congress to organize, arm, and discipline the militia, it did not prevent Congress from providing for the militia's *dis*armament....

---

13. The Court notes that the *First Amendment* protects two separate rights with the phrase "the 'right [singular] of the people peaceably to assemble, and to petition the Government for a redress of grievances.'" *Ante*, at 18. But this only proves the point: In contrast to the language quoted by the Court, the Second Amendment does not protect a "right to keep *and to* bear arms," but rather a "right to keep and bear arms." The state constitutions cited by the Court are distinguishable on the same ground.

[This risk] was one of the primary objections to the original Constitution voiced by its opponents. The Anti-Federalists were ultimately unsuccessful in persuading state ratification conventions to condition their approval of the Constitution upon the eventual inclusion of any particular amendment. But a number of States did propose to the first Federal Congress amendments reflecting a desire to ensure that the institution of the militia would remain protected under the new Government. [While some proposals] were exclusively concerned with standing armies and conscientious objectors, [others] would have protected a more broadly worded right, less clearly tied to service in a state militia. Faced with all of these options, it is telling that James Madison chose to craft the Second Amendment as he did....

Madison's decision to model the Second Amendment on the distinctly military [proposal] is therefore revealing, since it is clear that he considered and rejected formulations that would have unambiguously protected civilian uses of firearms. When Madison prepared his first draft, and when that draft was debated and modified, it is reasonable to assume that all participants in the drafting process were fully aware of the other formulations that would have protected civilian use and possession of weapons and that their choice to craft the Amendment as they did represented a rejection of those alternative formulations.

Madison's initial inclusion of an exemption for conscientious objectors sheds revelatory light on the purpose of the Amendment. It confirms an intent to describe a duty as well as a right, and it unequivocally identifies the military character of both....

III

Although it gives short shrift to the drafting history of the Second Amendment, the Court dwells at length on four other sources: the 17th-century English Bill of Rights; Blackstone's Commentaries on the Laws of England; postenactment commentary on the Second Amendment; and post-Civil War legislative history. All of these sources shed only indirect light on the question before us, and in any event offer little support for the Court's conclusion.

The English Bill of Rights

The Court's reliance on Article VII of the 1689 English Bill of Rights—which, like most of the evidence offered by the Court today, was considered in *Miller*—is misguided both because Article VII was enacted in response to different concerns from those that motivated the Framers of the Second Amendment, and because the guarantees of the two provisions were by no means coextensive. Moreover, the English text contained no preamble or other provision identifying a narrow, militia-related purpose.

The English Bill of Rights responded to abuses by the Stuart monarchs; among the grievances set forth in the Bill of Rights was that the King had violated the law "[b]y causing several good Subjects being Protestants to be disarmed at the same time when Papists were both armed and Employed contrary to Law." Article VII of the Bill of Rights was a response to that selective disarmament; it guaranteed that "the Subjects which are Protestants may have Armes for their defence, Suitable to their condition and as allowed by Law." This grant did not establish a general right of all persons, or even of all Protestants, to possess weapons. Rather, the right was qualified in two distinct ways: First, it was restricted to those of adequate social and economic status ("suitable to their Condition"); second, it was only available subject to regulation by Parliament ("as allowed by Law").

The Court may well be correct that the English Bill of Rights protected the right of *some* English subjects to use *some* arms for personal self-defense free from restrictions by the Crown (but not Parliament). But that right—adopted in a different historical and political context and framed in markedly different language—tells us little about the meaning of the Second Amendment.

Blackstone's Commentaries

The Court's reliance on Blackstone's Commentaries on the Laws of England is unpersuasive for the same reason as its reliance on the English Bill of Rights. Blackstone's invocation of "'the natural right of resistance and self-preservation,'" and "'the right of having and using arms for self-preservation and defence'" referred specifically to Article VII in the English Bill of Rights. The excerpt from Blackstone offered by the Court, therefore, is, like Article VII itself, of limited use in interpreting the very differently worded, and differently historically situated, Second Amendment.

What *is* important about Blackstone is the instruction he provided on reading the sort of text before us today. Blackstone described an interpretive approach that gave far more weight to preambles than the Court allows.... "[T]he proeme, or preamble, is often called in to help the construction of an act of parliament."

Postenactment Commentary

The Court also excerpts, without any real analysis, commentary by a number of additional scholars, some near in time to the framing and others post-dating it by close to a century. Those scholars are for the most part of limited relevance in construing the guarantee of the Second Amendment: Their views are not altogether clear, they tended to collapse the Second Amendment with Article VII of the English Bill of Rights, and they appear to have been unfamiliar with the drafting history of the Second Amendment....

Post-Civil War Legislative History

The Court suggests that by the post-Civil War period, the Second Amendment was understood to secure a right to firearm use and ownership for purely private purposes like personal self-defense. While it is true that some of the legislative history on which the Court relies supports that contention, such sources are entitled to limited, if any, weight. All of the statements the Court cites were made long after the framing of the Amendment and cannot possibly supply any insight into the intent of the Framers; and all were made during pitched political debates, so that they are better characterized as advocacy than good-faith attempts at constitutional interpretation.

What is more, much of the evidence the Court offers is decidedly less clear than its discussion allows. The Court notes that "[b]lacks were routinely disarmed by Southern States after the Civil War. Those who opposed these injustices frequently stated that they infringed blacks' constitutional right to keep and bear arms." The Court hastily concludes that "[n]eedless to say, the claim was not that blacks were being prohibited from carrying arms in an organized state militia." But some of the claims of the sort the Court cites may have been just that. In some Southern States, Reconstruction-era Republican governments created state militias in which both blacks and whites were permitted to serve. Because "[t]he decision to allow blacks to serve alongside whites meant that most southerners refused to join the new militia," the bodies were dubbed "Negro militia[s]."....

IV....

[The Second] Amendment played little role in any legislative debate about the civilian use of firearms for most of the 19th century, and it made few appearances in the decisions of this Court. Two 19th-century cases, however, bear mentioning.

In *United States v. Cruikshank*, 92 U.S. 542 (1876), the Court sustained a challenge to respondents' convictions under the Enforcement Act of 1870 for conspiring to deprive any individual of "'any right or privilege granted or secured to him by the constitution or laws of the United States.'" The Court wrote, as to counts 2 and 10 of respondents' indictment:"

> The right there specified is that of "'bearing arms for a lawful purpose." This is not a right granted by the Constitution. Neither is it in any manner dependent on that instrument for its existence. The Second amendment declares that it shall not be infringed; but this, as has been seen, means no more than that it shall not be infringed by Congress. This is one of the amendments that has no other effect than to restrict the powers of the national government.

The majority's assertion that the Court in *Cruikshank* "described the right protected by the Second Amendment as "'bearing arms for a lawful purpose,'" is not accurate. The *Cruikshank* Court explained that the defective *indictment* contained such language, but the Court did not itself describe the right, or endorse the indictment's description of the right....

Only one other 19th-century case in this Court, *Presser v. Illinois*, 116 U.S. 252 (1886), engaged in any significant discussion of the Second Amendment. The petitioner in *Presser* was convicted of violating a state statute that prohibited organizations other than the Illinois National Guard from associating together as military companies or parading with arms. Presser challenged his conviction, asserting, as relevant, that the statute violated both the Second and the Fourteenth Amendments....

[In upholding the conviction,] *Presser,* therefore, both affirmed *Cruikshank*'s holding that the Second Amendment posed no obstacle to regulation by state governments, and suggested that in any event nothing in the Constitution protected the use of arms outside the context of a militia "authorized by law" and organized by the State or Federal Government....

[The] dominant understanding of the Second Amendment's inapplicability to private gun ownership continued well into the 20th century. The first two federal laws directly restricting civilian use and possession of firearms—the 1927 Act prohibiting mail delivery of "pistols, revolvers, and other firearms capable of being concealed on the person," and the 1934 Act prohibiting the possession of sawed-off shotguns and machine guns—were enacted over minor Second Amendment objections dismissed by the vast majority of the legislators who participated in the debates. Members of Congress clashed over the wisdom and efficacy of such laws as crime-control measures. But since the statutes did not infringe upon the military use or possession of weapons, for most legislators they did not even raise the specter of possible conflict with the Second Amendment.

Thus, for most of our history, the invalidity of Second-Amendment-based objections to firearms regulations has been well settled and uncontroversial.[38]

---

38. The majority appears to suggest that even if the meaning of the Second Amendment has been considered settled by courts and legislatures for over two centuries, that settled meaning is overcome by the "reliance of millions of Americans" "upon the true meaning of the right to keep and bear arms." Presumably by this the Court means that many Americans own guns for self-defense, recreation, and other lawful purposes, and object to government interference with their gun ownership. I do not dispute the correctness of this observation. But it is hard to see how Americans have "relied," in the usual sense of the word, on the existence of a constitutional right that, until 2001, had been rejected by every federal court to take up the question. Rather, gun owners have "relied" on the laws passed by democratically elected legislatures, which have generally adopted only limited gun-control measures.

Indeed, the Second Amendment was not even mentioned in either full House of Congress during the legislative proceedings that led to the passage of the 1934 Act. Yet enforcement of that law produced the judicial decision that confirmed the status of the Amendment as limited in reach to military usage. After reviewing many of the same sources that are discussed at greater length by the Court today, the *Miller* Court unanimously concluded that the Second Amendment did not apply to the possession of a firearm that did not have "some reasonable relationship to the preservation or efficiency of a well regulated militia."

The key to that decision did not, as the Court belatedly suggests, turn on the difference between muskets and sawed-off shotguns; it turned, rather, on the basic difference between the military and nonmilitary use and possession of guns. Indeed, if the Second Amendment were not limited in its coverage to military uses of weapons, why should the Court in *Miller* have suggested that some weapons but not others were eligible for Second Amendment protection? If use for self-defense were the relevant standard, why did the Court not inquire into the suitability of a particular weapon for self-defense purposes?

Perhaps in recognition of the weakness of its attempt to distinguish *Miller*, the Court argues in the alternative that *Miller* should be discounted because of its decisional history. It is true that the appellee in *Miller* did not file a brief or make an appearance, although the court below had held that the relevant provision of the National Firearms Act violated the Second Amendment (albeit without any reasoned opinion). But, as our decision in *Marbury v. Madison*, 5 U.S. 137, in which only one side appeared and presented arguments, demonstrates, the absence of adversarial presentation alone is not a basis for refusing to accord *stare decisis* effect to a decision of this Court....

The majority cannot seriously believe that the *Miller* Court did not consider any relevant evidence; the majority simply does not approve of the conclusion the *Miller* Court reached on that evidence. Standing alone, that is insufficient reason to disregard a unanimous opinion of this Court, upon which substantial reliance has been placed by legislators and citizens for nearly 70 years.

Indeed, reliance interests surely cut the other way: Even apart from the reliance of judges and legislators who properly believed, until today, that the Second Amendment did not reach possession of firearms for purely private activities, "millions of Americans," have relied on the power of government to protect their safety and well-being, and that of their families. With respect to the case before us, the legislature of the District of Columbia has relied on its ability to act to "reduce the potentiality for gun-related crimes and gun-related deaths from occurring within the District of Columbia," H. Con. Res. 694, 94th Cong., 2d Sess., 25 (1976); so, too have the residents of the District.

V

The Court concludes its opinion by declaring that it is not the proper role of this Court to change the meaning of rights "enshrine[d]" in the Constitution. But the right the Court announces was not "enshrined" in the Second Amendment by the Framers; it is the product of today's law-changing decision. The majority's exegesis has utterly failed to establish that as a matter of text or history, "the right of law-abiding, responsible citizens to use arms in defense of hearth and home" is "elevate[d] above all other interests" by the Second Amendment.

Until today, it has been understood that legislatures may regulate the civilian use and misuse of firearms so long as they do not interfere with the preservation of a well-regulated militia. The Court's announcement of a new constitutional right to own and use firearms for private purposes upsets that settled understanding, but leaves for future cases the formidable task of defining the scope of permissible regulations. Today judicial craftsmen have confidently asserted that a policy choice that denies a "law-abiding, responsible citize[n]" the right to keep and use weapons in the home for self-defense is "off the table." Given the presumption that most citizens are law abiding, and the reality that the need to defend oneself may suddenly arise in a host of locations outside the home, I fear that the District's policy choice may well be just the first of an unknown number of dominoes to be knocked off the table.[39]

[Today's decision] will surely give rise to a far more active judicial role in making vitally important national policy decisions than was envisioned at any time in the 18th, 19th, or 20th centuries.

The Court properly disclaims any interest in evaluating the wisdom of the specific policy choice challenged in this case, but it fails to pay heed to a far more important policy choice—the choice made by the Framers themselves. The Court would have us believe that over 200 years ago, the Framers made a choice to limit the tools available to elected officials wishing to regulate civilian

---

39. It was just a few years after the decision in *Miller* that Justice Frankfurter (by any measure a true judicial conservative) warned of the perils that would attend this Court's entry into the "political thicket" of legislative districting. *Colegrove v. Green*, 328 U.S. 549 (1946) (plurality opinion). The equally controversial political thicket that the Court has decided to enter today is qualitatively different from the one that concerned Justice Frankfurter: While our entry into that thicket was justified because the political process was manifestly unable to solve the problem of unequal districts, no one has suggested that the political process is not working exactly as it should in mediating the debate between the advocates and opponents of gun control. What impact the Court's unjustified entry into *this* thicket will have on that ongoing debate—or indeed on the Court itself—is a matter that future historians will no doubt discuss at length. It is, however, clear to me that adherence to a policy of judicial restraint would be far wiser than the bold decision announced today.

uses of weapons, and to authorize this Court to use the common-law process of case-by-case judicial lawmaking to define the contours of acceptable gun control policy. Absent compelling evidence that is nowhere to be found in the Court's opinion, I could not possibly conclude that the Framers made such a choice.

For these reasons, I respectfully dissent.

JUSTICE BREYER, with whom JUSTICE STEVENS, JUSTICE SOUTER, and JUSTICE GINSBURG join, dissenting. . . .

I

The majority's conclusion is wrong for two independent reasons. The first reason is that set forth by Justice Stevens — namely, that the Second Amendment protects militia-related, not self-defense-related, interests. . . .

The second independent reason is that the protection the Amendment provides is not absolute. The Amendment permits government to regulate the interests that it serves. Thus, irrespective of what those interests are — whether they do or do not include an independent interest in self-defense — the majority's view cannot be correct unless it can show that the District's regulation is unreasonable or inappropriate in Second Amendment terms. This the majority cannot do. . . .

II. . . .

[Colonial] history itself offers important examples of the kinds of gun regulation that citizens would then have thought compatible with the "right to keep and bear arms," whether embodied in Federal or State Constitutions, or the background common law. And those examples include substantial regulation of firearms in urban areas, including regulations that imposed obstacles to the use of firearms for the protection of the home. . . .

This historical evidence demonstrates that a self-defense assumption is the *beginning*, rather than the *end*, of any constitutional inquiry. That the District law impacts self-defense merely raises *questions* about the law's constitutionality. [There] are no purely logical or conceptual answers to such questions. All of which to say that to raise a self-defense question is not to answer it.

III

I therefore begin by asking a process-based question: How is a court to determine whether a particular firearm regulation (here, the District's restriction on handguns) is consistent with the Second Amendment? What kind of constitutional standard should the court use? How high a protective hurdle does the Amendment erect?

The question matters. The majority is wrong when it says that the District's law is unconstitutional "[u]nder any of the standards of scrutiny that we have applied to enumerated constitutional rights." How could that be? It certainly would not be unconstitutional under, for example, a "rational basis" standard, which requires a court to uphold regulation so long as it bears a "rational relationship" to a "legitimate governmental purpose." The law at issue here, which in part seeks to prevent gun-related accidents, at least bears a "rational relationship" to that "legitimate" life-saving objective....

Respondent proposes that the Court adopt a "strict scrutiny" test, which would require reviewing with care each gun law to determine whether it is "narrowly tailored to achieve a compelling governmental interest." But the majority implicitly, and appropriately, rejects that suggestion by broadly approving a set of laws — prohibitions on concealed weapons, forfeiture by criminals of the Second Amendment right, prohibitions on firearms in certain locales, and governmental regulation of commercial firearm sales — whose constitutionality under a strict scrutiny standard would be far from clear.

Indeed, adoption of a true strict-scrutiny standard for evaluating gun regulations would be impossible. That is because almost every gun-control regulation will seek to advance (as the one here does) a "primary concern of every government — a concern for the safety and indeed the lives of its citizens." *United States v. Salerno*, 481 U.S. 739 (1987). The Court has deemed that interest, as well as "the Government's general interest in preventing crime," to be "compelling," and the Court has in a wide variety of constitutional contexts found such public-safety concerns sufficiently forceful to justify restrictions on individual liberties, see *e.g.*, *Brandenburg v. Ohio*, 395 U.S. 444 (1969) (per curiam) (First Amendment free speech rights); *Sherbert v. Verner*, 374 U.S. 398 (1963) (First Amendment religious rights); *Brigham City v. Stuart*, 547 U.S. 398 (2006) (Fourth Amendment protection of the home); *New York v. Quarles*, 467 U.S. 649 (1984) (Fifth Amendment rights under *Miranda v. Arizona*); *Salerno*, *supra* (Eighth Amendment bail rights). Thus, any attempt *in theory* to apply strict scrutiny to gun regulations will *in practice* turn into an interest-balancing inquiry, with the interests protected by the Second Amendment on one side and the governmental public-safety concerns on the other, the only question being whether the regulation at issue impermissibly burdens the former in the course of advancing the latter.

I would simply adopt such an interest-balancing inquiry explicitly....

In applying this kind of standard the Court normally defers to a legislature's empirical judgment in matters where a legislature is likely to have greater expertise and greater institutional factfinding capacity....

The above-described approach seems preferable to a more rigid approach here for a further reason. Experience as much as logic has led the Court to decide that in one area of constitutional law or another the interests are likely to prove stronger on one side of a typical constitutional case than on the other. Here, we have little prior experience. Courts that *do* have experience in these matters have uniformly taken an approach that treats empirically-based legislative judgment with a degree of deference....

IV....

[Justice Breyer turns now to the constitutionality of the District's ban on handguns.]

A

No one doubts the constitutional importance of the statute's basic objective, saving lives. But there is considerable debate about whether the District's statute helps to achieve that objective. I begin by reviewing the statute's tendency to secure that objective from the perspective of (1) the legislature (namely, the Council of the District of Columbia) that enacted the statute in 1976, and (2) a court that seeks to evaluate the Council's decision today.

1

First, consider the facts as the legislature saw them when it adopted the District statute. As stated by the local council committee that recommended its adoption, the major substantive goal of the District's handgun restriction is "to reduce the potentiality for gun-related crimes and gun-related deaths from occurring within the District of Columbia." The committee concluded, on the basis of "extensive public hearings" and "lengthy research," that "[t]he easy availability of firearms in the United States has been a major factor contributing to the drastic increase in gun-related violence and crime over the past 40 years." It reported to the Council "startling statistics," regarding gun-related crime, accidents, and deaths, focusing particularly on the relation between handguns and crime and the proliferation of handguns within the District.

The committee informed the Council that guns were "responsible for 69 deaths in this country each day," for a total of "[a]pproximately 25,000 gun-deaths... each year," along with an additional 200,000 gun-related injuries. Three thousand of these deaths, the report stated, were accidental. A quarter of the victims in those accidental deaths were children under the age of 14. And according to the committee, "[f]or every intruder stopped by a homeowner with a firearm, there are 4 gun-related accidents within the home."

In respect to local crime, the committee observed that there were 285 murders in the District during 1974—a record number. The committee also stated that, "[c]ontrary to popular opinion on the subject, firearms are more frequently involved in deaths and violence among relatives and friends than in premeditated criminal activities." Citing an article from the American Journal of Psychiatry, the committee reported that "[m]ost murders are committed by previously law-abiding citizens, in situations where spontaneous violence is generated by anger, passion or intoxication, and where the killer and victim are acquainted." "Twenty-five percent of these murders," the committee informed the Council, "occur within families."

The committee report furthermore presented statistics strongly correlating handguns with crime. Of the 285 murders in the District in 1974, 155 were committed with handguns. This did not appear to be an aberration, as the report revealed that "handguns [had been] used in roughly 54% of all murders" (and 87% of murders of law enforcement officers) nationwide over the preceding several years. Nor were handguns only linked to murders, as statistics showed that they were used in roughly 60% of robberies and 26% of assaults. "A crime committed with a pistol," the committee reported, "is 7 times more likely to be lethal than a crime committed with any other weapon."...

The District's special focus on handguns thus reflects the fact that the committee report found them to have a particularly strong link to undesirable activities in the District's exclusively urban environment. The District did not seek to prohibit possession of other sorts of weapons deemed more suitable for an "urban area."

2

Next, consider the facts as a court must consider them looking at the matter as of today. Petitioners, and their *amici,* have presented us with more recent statistics that tell much the same story that the committee report told 30 years ago. At the least, they present nothing that would permit us to second-guess the Council in respect to the numbers of gun crimes, injuries, and deaths, or the role of handguns.

From 1993 to 1997, there were 180,533 firearm-related deaths in the United States, an average of over 36,000 per year. Fifty-one percent were suicides, 44% were homicides, 1% were legal interventions, 3% were unintentional accidents, and 1% were of undetermined causes. Over that same period there were an additional 411,800 nonfatal firearm-related injuries treated in U.S. hospitals, an average of over 82,000 per year. Of these, 62% resulted from assaults, 17% were unintentional, 6% were suicide attempts, 1% were legal interventions, and 13% were of unknown causes.

The statistics are particularly striking in respect to children and adolescents. In over one in every eight firearm-related deaths in 1997, the victim was someone under the age of 20. Firearm-related deaths account for 22.5% of all injury deaths between the ages of 1 and 19. More male teenagers die from firearms than from all natural causes combined.

Handguns are involved in a majority of firearm deaths and injuries in the United States. From 1993 to 1997, 81% of firearm-homicide victims were killed by handgun. In the same period, for the 41% of firearm injuries for which the weapon type is known, 82% of them were from handguns. And among children under the age of 20, handguns account for approximately 70% of all unintentional firearm-related injuries and deaths....

Handguns also appear to be a very popular weapon among criminals. In a 1997 survey of inmates who were armed during the crime for which they were incarcerated, 83.2% of state inmates and 86.7% of federal inmates said that they were armed with a handgun. And handguns are not only popular tools for crime, but popular objects of it as well: the FBI received on average over 274,000 reports of stolen guns for each year between 1985 and 1994, and almost 60% of stolen guns are handguns. Department of Justice studies have concluded that stolen handguns in particular are an important source of weapons for both adult and juvenile offenders.

Statistics further suggest that urban areas, such as the District, have different experiences with gun-related death, injury, and crime, than do less densely populated rural areas. A disproportionate amount of violent and property crimes occur in urban areas, and urban criminals are more likely than other offenders to use a firearm during the commission of a violent crime....

3

Respondent and his many *amici* for the most part do not disagree about the *figures* set forth in the preceding subsection, but they do disagree strongly with the District's *predictive judgment* that a ban on handguns will help solve the crime and accident problems that those figures disclose....

First, they point out that, since the ban took effect, violent crime in the District has increased, not decreased. Indeed, a comparison with 49 other major cities reveals that the District's homicide rate is actually substantially *higher* relative to these other cities than it was before the handgun restriction went into effect.

Second, respondent's *amici* point to a statistical analysis that regresses murder rates against the presence or absence of strict gun laws in 20 European nations. That analysis concludes that strict gun laws are correlated with *more* murders, not fewer. They further argue that handgun bans do not reduce suicide rates, or rates of accidents, even those involving children.

Third, they point to evidence indicating that firearm ownership does have a beneficial self-defense effect. Based on a 1993 survey, the authors of one study estimated that there were 2.2-to-2.5 million defensive uses of guns (mostly brandishing, about a quarter involving the actual firing of a gun) annually. Another study estimated that for a period of 12 months ending in 1994, there were 503,481 incidents in which a burglar found himself confronted by an armed homeowner, and that in 497,646 (98.8%) of them, the intruder was successfully scared away. A third study suggests that gun-armed victims are substantially less likely than non-gun-armed victims to be injured in resisting robbery or assault. And additional evidence suggests that criminals are likely to be deterred from burglary and other crimes if they know the victim is likely to have a gun.

Fourth, respondent's *amici* argue that laws criminalizing gun possession are self-defeating, as evidence suggests that they will have the effect only of restricting law-abiding citizens, but not criminals, from acquiring guns....

These empirically based arguments may have proved strong enough to convince many legislatures, as a matter of legislative policy, not to adopt total handgun bans. But the question here is whether they are strong enough to destroy judicial confidence in the reasonableness of a legislature that rejects them. And that they are not. For one thing, they can lead us more deeply into the uncertainties that surround any effort to reduce crime, but they cannot prove either that handgun possession diminishes crime or that handgun bans are ineffective. The statistics do show a soaring District crime rate. And the District's crime rate went up after the District adopted its handgun ban. But, as students of elementary logic know, *after it* does not mean *because of it*. What would the District's crime rate have looked like without the ban? Higher? Lower? The same? Experts differ; and we, as judges, cannot say.

What about the fact that foreign nations with strict gun laws have higher crime rates? Which is the cause and which the effect? The proposition that strict gun laws *cause* crime is harder to accept than the proposition that strict gun laws in part grow out of the fact that a nation already has a higher crime rate. And we are then left with the same question as before: What would have happened to crime without the gun laws—a question that respondent and his *amici* do not convincingly answer.

Further, suppose that respondent's *amici* are right when they say that householders' possession of loaded handguns help to frighten away intruders. On that assumption, one must still ask whether that benefit is worth the potential death-related cost. And that is a question without a directly provable answer.

Finally, consider the claim of respondent's *amici* that handgun bans *cannot* work; there are simply too many illegal guns already in existence for a ban on legal guns to make a difference. In a word, they claim that, given the urban sea of pre-existing legal guns, criminals can readily find arms regardless. Nonetheless, a legislature might respond, we want to make an effort to try to dry up that urban sea, drop by drop. And none of the studies can show that effort is not worthwhile.

In a word, the studies to which respondent's *amici* point raise policy-related questions. They succeed in proving that the District's predictive judgments are controversial. But they do not by themselves show that those judgments are incorrect; nor do they demonstrate a consensus, academic or otherwise, supporting that conclusion.

Thus, it is not surprising that the District and its *amici* support the District's handgun restriction with studies of their own. One in particular suggests that, statistically speaking, the District's law has indeed had positive life-saving effects. Others suggest that firearm restrictions as a general matter reduce homicides, suicides, and accidents in the home. Still others suggest that the defensive uses of handguns are not as great in number as respondent's *amici* claim....

The upshot is a set of studies and counterstudies that, at most, could leave a judge uncertain about the proper policy conclusion. But from respondent's perspective any such uncertainty is not good enough. That is because legislators, not judges, have primary responsibility for drawing policy conclusions from empirical fact. And, given that constitutional allocation of decisionmaking responsibility, the empirical evidence presented here is sufficient to allow a judge to reach a firm *legal* conclusion....

[T]he District's decision represents the kind of empirically based judgment that legislatures, not courts, are best suited to make. In fact, deference to legislative judgment seems particularly appropriate here, where the judgment has been made by a local legislature, with particular knowledge of local problems and insight into appropriate local solutions....

B

I next assess the extent to which the District's law burdens the interests that the Second Amendment seeks to protect....

1

The District's statute burdens the Amendment's first and primary objective [of protecting the militia] hardly at all....

To begin with, the present case has nothing to do with *actual* military service. [I] am aware of no indication that the District either now or in the recent past has called up its citizenry to serve in a militia, that it has any inkling of doing so anytime in the foreseeable future, or that this law must be construed to prevent the use of handguns during legitimate militia activities....

[The] District's law does not seriously affect military training interests. The law permits residents to engage in activities that will increase their familiarity with firearms. They may register (and thus possess in their homes) weapons other than handguns, such as rifles and shotguns. See D. C. Code §§ 7-2502.01, 7-2502.02(a) (only weapons that cannot be registered are sawed-off shotguns, machine guns, short-barreled rifles, and pistols not registered before 1976)....

And while the District law prevents citizens from training with handguns *within the District*, the District consists of only 61.4 square miles of urban area. The adjacent States do permit the use of handguns for target practice, and those States are only a brief subway ride away....

Of course, a subway rider must buy a ticket, and the ride takes time. It also costs money to store a pistol, say, at a target range, outside the District. But given the costs already associated with gun ownership and firearms training, I cannot say that a subway ticket and a short subway ride (and storage costs) create more than a minimal burden. Compare *Crawford v. Marion County Election Bd.*, 553 U.S. ____ (2008) (Breyer, J., dissenting) (acknowledging travel burdens on indigent persons in the context of voting where public transportation options were limited)....

2

The majority briefly suggests that the "right to keep and bear Arms" might encompass an interest in hunting. But in enacting the present provisions, the District sought "to take nothing away from sportsmen." And any inability of District residents to hunt near where they live has much to do with the jurisdiction's exclusively urban character and little to do with the District's firearm laws....

3

The District's law does prevent a resident from keeping a loaded handgun in his home. And it consequently makes it more difficult for the householder to use the handgun for self-defense in the home against intruders, such as burglars. [Statistics] suggest that handguns are the most popular weapon for self-defense. And there are some legitimate reasons why that would be the case. [To] that extent the law burdens to some degree an interest in self-defense that for present purposes I have assumed the Amendment seeks to further.

C

In weighing needs and burdens, we must take account of the possibility that there are reasonable, but less restrictive alternatives. Are there *other* potential measures that might similarly promote the same goals while imposing lesser restrictions? Here I see none.

The reason there is no clearly superior, less restrictive alternative to the District's handgun ban is that the ban's very objective is to reduce significantly the number of handguns in the District, say, for example, by allowing a law enforcement officer immediately to assume that *any* handgun he sees is an *illegal* handgun. And there is no plausible way to achieve that objective other than to ban the guns....

[Any] measure less restrictive in respect to the use of handguns for self-defense will, to that same extent, prove less effective in preventing the use of handguns for illicit purposes. If a resident has a handgun in the home that he can use for self-defense, then he has a handgun in the home that he can use to commit suicide or engage in acts of domestic violence. . . .

Licensing restrictions would not similarly reduce the handgun population, and the District may reasonably fear that even if guns are initially restricted to law-abiding citizens, they might be stolen and thereby placed in the hands of criminals. . . .

The absence of equally effective alternatives to a complete prohibition finds support in the empirical fact that other States and urban centers prohibit particular types of weapons. . . .

D

The upshot is that the District's objectives are compelling; its predictive judgments as to its law's tendency to achieve those objectives are adequately supported; the law does impose a burden upon any self-defense interest that the Amendment seeks to secure; and there is no clear less restrictive alternative. I turn now to the final portion of the "permissible regulation" question: Does the District's law *disproportionately* burden Amendment-protected interests? Several considerations, taken together, convince me that it does not.

First, the District law is tailored to the life-threatening problems it attempts to address. The law concerns one class of weapons, handguns, leaving residents free to possess shotguns and rifles, along with ammunition. The area that falls within its scope is totally urban.

Second, the self-defense interest in maintaining loaded handguns in the home to shoot intruders is not the *primary* interest, but at most a subsidiary interest, that the Second Amendment seeks to serve. . . .

Further, any self-defense interest at the time of the Framing could not have focused exclusively upon urban-crime related dangers. Two hundred years ago, most Americans, many living on the frontier, would likely have thought of self-defense primarily in terms of outbreaks of fighting with Indian tribes, rebellions such as Shays' Rebellion, marauders, and crime-related dangers to travelers on the roads, on footpaths, or along waterways. Insofar as the Framers focused at all on the tiny fraction of the population living in large cities, they would have been aware that these city dwellers were subject to firearm restrictions that their rural counterparts were not. They are unlikely then to have thought of a right to keep loaded handguns in homes to confront intruders in urban settings as *central*. . . .

Nor, for that matter, am I aware of any evidence that *handguns* in particular were central to the Framers' conception of the Second Amendment. The lists of militia-related weapons in the late 18th-century state statutes appear primarily to refer to other sorts of weapons, muskets in particular. . . .

Third, irrespective of what the Framers *could have thought,* we know what they *did think.* Samuel Adams, who lived in Boston, advocated a constitutional amendment that would have precluded the Constitution from ever being "construed" to "prevent the people of the United States, who are peaceable citizens, from keeping their own arms." Samuel Adams doubtless knew that the Massachusetts Constitution contained somewhat similar protection. And he doubtless knew that Massachusetts law prohibited Bostonians from keeping loaded guns in the house. So how could Samuel Adams have advocated such protection *unless* he thought that the protection was *consistent* with local regulation that seriously impeded urban residents from using their arms against intruders? It seems unlikely that he meant to deprive the Federal Government of power (to enact Boston-type weapons regulation) that he know Boston had and (as far as we know) he would have thought constitutional under the Massachusetts Constitution. . . .

Fourth, a contrary view, as embodied in today's decision, will have unfortunate consequences. The decision will encourage legal challenges to gun regulation throughout the Nation. Because it says little about the standards used to evaluate regulatory decisions, it will leave the Nation without clear standards for resolving those challenges. And litigation over the course of many years, or the mere specter of such litigation, threatens to leave cities without effective protection against gun violence and accidents during that time. . . .

V

The majority derides my approach as "judge-empowering." I take this criticism seriously, but I do not think it accurate. . . .

The majority's methodology is, in my view, substantially less transparent than mine. At a minimum, I find it difficult to understand the reasoning that seems to underlie certain conclusions that it reaches.

The majority spends the first 54 pages of its opinion attempting to rebut Justice Stevens' evidence that the Amendment was enacted with a purely militia-related purpose. In the majority's view, the Amendment also protects an interest in armed personal self-defense, at least to some degree. But the majority does not tell us precisely what that interest is. "Putting all of [the Second Amendment's] textual elements together," the majority says, "we find that they guarantee the individual right to possess and carry weapons in case of confrontation." Then, three pages later, it says that "we do not read the Second Amendment to permit citizens to carry arms for *any sort* of confrontation." Yet, with one critical exception, it does not explain which confrontations count. It simply leaves that question unanswered.

The majority does, however, point to one type of confrontation that counts, for it describes the Amendment as "elevat[ing] above all other interests the right of law-abiding, responsible citizens to use arms in defense of hearth and home." What is its basis for finding that to be the core of the Second Amendment right? The only historical sources identified by the majority that even appear to touch upon that specific matter consist of an 1866 newspaper editorial discussing the Freedmen's Bureau Act, two quotations from that 1866 Act's legislative history, and a 1980 state court opinion saying that in colonial times the same were used to defend the home as to maintain the militia. How can citations such as these support the far-reaching proposition that the Second Amendment's primary concern is not its stated concern about the militia, but rather a right to keep loaded weapons at one's bedside to shoot intruders?

Nor is it at all clear to me how the majority decides *which* loaded "arms" a homeowner may keep. The majority says that that Amendment protects those weapons "typically possessed by law-abiding citizens for lawful purposes." This definition conveniently excludes machineguns, but permits handguns, which the majority describes as "the most popular weapon chosen by Americans for self-defense in the home." But what sense does this approach make? According to the majority's reasoning, if Congress and the States lift restrictions on the possession and use of machineguns, and people buy machineguns to protect their homes, the Court will have to reverse course and find that the Second Amendment *does*, in fact, protect the individual self-defense-related right to possess a machinegun. On the majority's reasoning, if tomorrow someone invents a particularly useful, highly dangerous self-defense weapon, Congress and the States had better ban it immediately, for once it becomes popular Congress will no longer possess the constitutional authority to do so. In essence, the majority determines what regulations are permissible by looking to see what existing regulations permit. There is no basis for believing that the Framers intended such circular reasoning.

I am similarly puzzled by the majority's list, in Part III of its opinion, of provisions that in its view would survive Second Amendment scrutiny. These consist of (1) "prohibitions on carrying concealed weapons"; (2) "prohibitions on the possession of firearms by felons"; (3) "prohibitions on the possession of firearms by... the mentally ill"; (4) "laws forbidding the carrying of firearms in sensitive places such as schools and government buildings"; and (5) government "conditions and qualifications" attached "to the commercial sale of arms." Why these? Is it that similar restrictions existed in the late 18th century? The majority fails to cite any colonial analogues....

At the same time the majority ignores a more important question: Given the purposes for which the Framers enacted the Second Amendment, how should it be applied to modern-day circumstances that they could not have anticipated? Assume, for argument's sake, that the Framers did intend the Amendment to offer a degree of self-defense protection. Does that mean that the Framers also intended to guarantee a right to possess a loaded gun near swimming pools, parks, and playgrounds? That they would not have cared about the children who might pick up a loaded gun on their parents' bedside table? That they (who certainly showed concern for the risk of fire) would have lacked concern for the risk of accidental deaths or suicides that readily accessible loaded handguns in urban areas might bring? Unless we believe that they intended future generations to ignore such matters, answering questions such as the questions in this case requires judgment—judicial judgment exercised within a framework for constitutional analysis that guides that judgment and which makes its exercise transparent. One cannot answer those questions by combining inconclusive historical research with judicial *ipse dixit*....

F. "Case or Controversy" Requirements and the Passive Virtues

Page 117. At the end of section 3a of the Note, add the following:

Compare *Sierra Club* and *SCRAP* to Summers v. Earth Island Institute, 129 S. Ct. 1142 (2009). Plaintiffs, a group of environmental organizations, challenged the failure of the United States Forest Service to enforce regulations requiring it to establish notice, comment, and appeal procedures for proposed actions implementing land and resource management plans. The Forest Service regulations provided for a categorical exemption from this requirement for fire-rehabilitation activities in relatively small areas that did not cause significant environmental impact.

Plaintiff's original action challenged the Forest Service's failure to provide for notice and comment with regard to a particular project. Soon after the District Court granted a preliminary injunction with regard to that project, the dispute over it was settled. Despite the fact that no other particular project was before the Court, the trial court held that the Forest Service regulations pertaining to that project were unlawful, and the Court of Appeals affirmed. In a five-to-four decision, the Supreme Court, in an opinion written by Justice Scalia, reversed.

The Court acknowledged that plaintiff organizations had standing to challenge the particular project, but rejected the proposition that when a "plaintiff has sued to challenge the lawfulness of certain action or threatened action but has settled that suit, he retains standing to challenge the basis for that action (here the regulation in the abstract), apart from any concrete application that threatens imminent harm to his interests." The plaintiffs lacked standing because they "have identified no other application of the invalidated regulations that threatens imminent and concrete harm to the interests of their members."

The Court held that an affidavit submitted by a member of one of the plaintiff organizations, alleging that he "has visited many National Forests and plans to visit several unnamed National Forests in the future" did not suffice. The affidavit failed

> to allege that *any* particular timber sale or other project claimed to be unlawfully subject to the regulations will impede a specific and concrete plan of [the affiant's] to enjoy the National Forests. The National Forests occupy more than 190 million acres, an area larger than Texas. There may be a chance, but it is hardly a likelihood, that [affiant's] wanderings will bring him to a parcel about to be affected by a project unlawfully subject to the regulations. Indeed, without further specification, it is impossible to tell *which* projects are (in respondents' view) unlawfully subject to regulations.

The Court also rejected plaintiffs' argument that they had standing to complain of the procedural injury caused by their inability to file comments on Forest Service actions. "[A] deprivation of a procedural right without some concrete interest that is affected by the deprivation — a procedural right *in vacuo* — is insufficient to create Article III standing." Nor was it relevant that the procedural right was created by Congress, since "the requirement of injury in fact is a hard floor of Article III jurisdiction that cannot be removed by statute."

In a short concurring opinion, Justice Kennedy joined the opinion of the Court, but noted that the case "would present different considerations if Congress had sought to provide redress for a concrete injury 'giv[ing] rise to a case or controversy where none existed before.'"

Justice Breyer filed a dissenting opinion that was joined by Justices Stevens, Souter, and Ginsburg. He observed that the plaintiff organizations had "hundreds of thousands of members who use forests regularly across the nation." The members' activities led him to this analogy: "To know, virtually for certain, that snow will fall in New England this winter is not to know the name of each particular town where it is bound to arrive. The law of standing does not require the latter kind of specificity."

Page 140. At the end of section 3 of the Note, add the following:

In Caperton v. A. T. Massey Coal Co., 129 S. Ct. 2252 (2009), the Supreme Court addressed the question whether the due process clause required a state supreme court justice to recuse himself from a case involving an individual who had spent roughly $3 million in support of the justice's election. In recent years, a number of litigants had raised questions regarding the propriety of elected judges — and more than forty states elect at least some of their judges — sitting on cases involving individuals who had made substantial expenditures in judicial election campaigns. The Supreme Court, by a five-to-four vote, held that under the circumstances of the case, due process required recusal. (The due process clause holding is described in more detail *infra* in the Supplement to page 960.)

Justice Kennedy's opinion for the Court concluded that recusal is required when "there is a serious risk of actual bias — based on objective and reasonable perceptions — [that] a person with a personal stake in a particular case had a significant and disproportionate influence in placing the judge on the case by raising funds or directing the judge's election campaign when the case was pending or imminent. The inquiry centers on the contribution's relative size in comparison to the total amount of money contributed to the campaign, the total amount spent in the election, and the apparent effect such contribution had on the outcome of the election." In the case before the Court, the Court found that Massey's chairman's efforts had had such influence. "His contributions eclipsed the total amount spent by all other [supporters] and exceeded by 300% the amount spent by [the justice's own] campaign committee."

The Court explained that:

> Our decision today addresses an extraordinary situation where the Constitution requires recusal. Massey and its *amici* predict that various adverse consequences will follow from recognizing a constitutional violation here — ranging from a flood of recusal motions to unnecessary interference with judicial elections. We disagree. The facts now before us are extreme by any measure. The parties point to no other instance involving judicial campaign contributions that presents a potential for bias comparable to the circumstances in this case.
>
> It is true that extreme cases often test the bounds of established legal principles, and sometimes no administrable standard may be available to address the perceived wrong. But it is also true that extreme cases are more likely to cross constitutional limits, requiring this Court's intervention and formulation of objective standards. This is particularly true when due process is violated. See, *e.g., County of Sacramento v. Lewis*, 523 U.S. 833 (1998) (reiterating the due-process prohibition on "executive abuse of power... which shocks the conscience"); id., at 858 (KENNEDY, J., concurring) (explaining that "objective considerations, including history and precedent, are the controlling principle" of this due process standard).

It concluded that because states' own codes of judicial conduct often required recusal under a wider range of circumstances and thus "provide more protection than due process requires, most disputes over disqualification will be resolved without resort to the Constitution. Application of the constitutional standard implicated in this case will thus be confined to rare instances."

In dissent, Chief Justice Roberts questioned whether the Court had identified any manageable standards for requiring recusal. He charged that "the standard the majority articulates [fails] to provide clear, workable guidance for future cases," and provided a numbered list of forty questions he claimed the Court's opinion left open, such as "How much money is too much money?," "Must the judge recuse in cases involving individuals or groups who spent large amounts of money trying unsuccessfully to defeat him?," and "If causation is a pertinent factor, how do we know whether the contribution or expenditure had any effect on the outcome of the election?" He concluded: "The Court's inability to formulate a 'judicially discernible and manageable standard' strongly counsels against the recognition of a novel constitutional right. See *Vieth v. Jubelirer*, 541 U.S. 267, 306 (2004) (plurality opinion) (holding political gerrymandering claims nonjusticiable based on the lack of workable standards); id., at 317 (KENNEDY, J., concurring in judgment) ('the failings of the many proposed standards for measuring the burden a gerrymander imposes... make our intervention improper.') The need to consider these and countless other questions helps explain why the common law and this Court's constitutional jurisprudence have never required disqualification on such vague grounds as 'probability' or 'appearance' of bias."

2
FEDERALISM AT WORK: CONGRESS AND THE NATIONAL ECONOMY

A. *The Values of Federalism and Some Techniques for Implementing Them*

Page 172. After section 6 of the Note, add the following:

6a. *A skeptical view of federalism's values.* Malcolm M. Feeley and Edward Rubin, Federalism: Political Identity and Tragic Compromise 15, 16 (2009), argue that federalism "serves as a means of modulating, or varying, political identity. [If] people's political identity is associated with some region that has been subsumed into a larger polity, federalism provides a means by which the disjunction between their political identity and their territorial mode of governance can be reduced. [Federalism] will only be appealing to people if the region itself [relates] to their sense of political identity." On this understanding, is federalism an appropriate form of governance for the United States?

Feely and Rubin distinguish federalism from decentralization and local democracy. Decentralization "is a managerial strategy by which a centralized regime can achieve the results it desires in a more effective manner." Id. at 20. So, for example, "if one wants to implement a program of ensuring and increasing participation in the democratic process, increasing the number of decentralized decisions may well be a valid way to proceed, but this would be a national policy, not a result of federalism. [Federalism] does not necessarily increase participation; it simply authorizes a set of specified political subunits to decide for themselves how much participation is desirable. Some might choose to encourage participation, but others might choose to suppress it." Id. at 22. They note that national policymakers could "achiev[e] the same goal [by] hiring community organizers, funding local organizations, and requiring approvals for government decisions from different sectors of the population," and that "[in] a truly federal regime, some states might opt for elections, while others might not." Id. at 22, 23. "Federalism reserves particular issues to subnational governmental units, regardless of the political process that exists within these units, whereas local democracy establishes a particular political process in the subnational units without granting those units any particular area of authority." Id. at 31. Similarly, experimentation is "a happy incident of managerial decentralization. [Divergent] goals will typically render instrumental experimentation irrelevant." Id. at 26.

On the argument that federalism promotes economic efficiency, Feeley and Rubin argue that "[federalism] allows a multiplicity of norms, not simply a multiplicity of rules. In a truly federal system, some subunits might not be interested in economic efficiency; [they] might be primarily motivated by the desire to preserve an agrarian lifestyle, to protect the environment, or to encourage individual spirituality. [They] might lose out in the competition for factories and corporate executives [but] rather than perceiving their losses as a chastening lesson [they] might perceive them as a necessary cost or as a positive advantage." Id. at 24.

On "the idea that people can choose among jurisdictions on the basis of the services that they provide," Feeley and Rubin argue that this "will be true [if] the national government imposes certain uniform standards [to] ensure that citizens can live as comfortably in one as in another [region] or [if] the nation is so culturally homogeneous that most of its citizens are comfortable in any of its regions." In the latter case, they argue, federalism "is unnecessary and thus likely to be vestigial." Id. at 24-25.

D. State Regulation of Interstate Commerce

Page 234. At the end of section 1a of the Note, add the following:

See also Erbsen, Horizontal Federalism, 93 Minn. L. Rev. 493, 503 (2008), which treats the dormant commerce doctrine as one of "a set of constitutional mechanisms for preventing or mitigating interstate friction that may arise from the out-of-state effects of in-state decisions." The full faith and credit clause and the article III provision for diversity jurisdiction are textual provisions in that set; the due process clause limitations on the assertion of state-court jurisdiction over out-of-state activity exemplify a doctrinal member of the set.

Page 238. At the end of section 3 of the Note, add the following:

See also Denning, Reconstructing the Dormant Commerce Clause Doctrine, 50 Wm. & Mary L. Rev. 417 (2008).

3
THE SCOPE OF CONGRESS'S POWERS: TAXING AND SPENDING, WAR POWERS, INDIVIDUAL RIGHTS, AND STATE AUTONOMY

A. *Regulation through Taxing, Spending, and the War Power*

Page 295. After section 4c of the Note, add the following:

To what extent do the limitations on Congress's powers under the commerce clause or the enforcement clauses of the Reconstruction-era amendments (particularly section 5 of the fourteenth amendment) carry over to the spending power? Consider N. Siegel, Dole's Future: A Strategic Analysis, 16 S. Ct. Econ. Rev. 165 (2008). Siegel identifies three different models of limitations on use of the spending clause. Under "substance federalism," the Court "conceives of the activity as concerning a matter that the Constitution leaves to the states." Id. at 191. Under "form federalism," the Court might "believ[e] a given regulation exceeds a particular congressional power, but would have no objection if Congress sought to accomplish the same goal through a different, legitimate source of authority. The Court, on that account, understands different constitutional 'hooks' for federal legislation to implicate distinct substantive values." Id. By contrast, under "form-plus-pique federalism," the Court might be "provoked by use of the Spending Clause after analogous use of the Commerce

Clause or Section Five had been struck down, even though the Court would not have been concerned about such use of the Spending Clause if a previous Commerce Clause or Section Five decision had not been rendered." Id. at 192. Siegel suggests that the members of the Roberts Court are potentially split among these positions:

> (1) Fewer than five votes exist for the view that advocates little or no judicially enforced federalism; (2) fewer than five votes likely exist for the substance federalism commitment; (3) fewer than five votes likely exist for the form federalism position; and (4) it is unclear how many Justices are appropriately characterized as form-plus-pique jurists. Because of (4), it is unclear (a) whether five votes exist for a combination of "no judicially enforced federalism" and form federalism, or (b) whether and when five votes likely exist for a combination of substance federalism and form plus pique.

Id. at 199.

Page 297. At the end of section 6 of the Note, add the following:

For a different view, see Galle, Federal Grants, State Decisions, 88 B.U.L. Rev. 875, 934 (2008) (arguing that the clear statement rule is indefensible in light of a variety of theoretical and empirical reasons to believe that state officials are not in fact constrained to accept federal grants and that the rule "displaces the expressed preferences of political actors, including both federal grant-offerors and state and local grant-acceptors").

C. The Tenth Amendment as a Federalism-Based Limitation on Congressional Power

Page 332. At the bottom of the page, after the first paragraph of section 3 of the Note, add the following:

See Vazquez, Missouri v. Holland's Second Holding, 73 Mo. L. Rev. 939, 967 (2008) (suggesting that Congress's treaty-making power may raise federalism concerns when Congress enters into "aspirational" treaties that concern matters that would otherwise lie outside Congress's Article I powers and suggesting a distinction between "obligatory treaties" and "aspirational" ones such that "the former treaties may be implemented by Congress even if they concern matters beyond Congress's legislative power under Article I, but the latter treaties may be implemented by Congress only if they concern matters within the Article I legislative power"). For a variety of views about the relationship between Congress's treaty power and the tenth amendment, see Symposium, Return to Missouri v. Holland: Federalism and International Law, 73 Mo. L. Rev. 921 (2008).

Page 349. At the end of section 1b of the Note, add the following:

In Haywood v. Drown, 129 S. Ct. 2108 (2009), the Supreme Court held that a New York statute that divested state courts of general jurisdiction of their power to hear damages actions under 42 U.S.C. § 1983 against state corrections officers — replacing those actions with the ability instead to sue the state itself in the New York Court of Claims, where the prisoner would not be entitled to attorney's fees, damages, or injunctive relief — violated the supremacy clause. The Court noted that under Testa v. Katt, a state could refuse jurisdiction on the basis of neutral rules regarding judicial administration, but found that New York's policy contradicted the congressional "judgment that *all* persons who violate federal rights while acting under color of state law shall be held liable for damages. As we have unanimously recognized, '[a] State may not . . . relieve congestion in its courts by declaring a whole category of federal claims to be frivolous.'"

4
THE DISTRIBUTION OF NATIONAL POWERS

A. *Introduction*

Page 357. At the end of section 2 of the Note, add the following:

Consider the possibility that by making the enactment of federal law difficult, separation of powers provisions serve to protect the values of federalism discussed in Chapters Two and Three, supra. For an argument along these lines, see Clark, Separation of Powers as a Safeguard of Federalism, 79 Tex. L. Rev. 1321 (2001). Compare Vazquez, The Separation of Powers as a Safeguard of Nationalism, 83 Notre Dame L. Rev. 1601, 1606 (2008) (arguing that "because the process of repealing a federal law is the same as for creating it in the first place, the requirements of bicameralism and presentment [can] make it difficult to restore legislative power [to] the states.")

B. *A Case Study: Presidential Seizure*

Page 370. At the end of section 2e of the Note, add the following:

Compare M. Tushnet, The Inevitable Globalization of Constitutional Law, 49 Va. J. Int'l L. 985, 988 (2009) (arguing that "because the globalization of domestic constitutional law is inevitable, notions of separation of powers — or of legislative supremacy qualified by the existence of judicial review — will need to accommodate themselves to that globalization.")

C. Foreign Affairs

Page 392. Before the Note, add the following:

For a survey of the obstacles imposed on defense lawyers representing Guantanamo detainees, including "policies designed to reduce their access to their clients; policies that create knotty ethical difficulties; [and] practices that ['are] designed to drive a wedge between lawyers and their clients,'" see Luban, Lawfare and Legal Ethics in Guantanamo, 60 Stan. L. Rev. 1981, 1983 (2008).

5
EQUALITY AND THE CONSTITUTION

C. Equal Protection Methodology: Heightened Scrutiny and the Problem of Race

Page 619. After section 3 of the Note, add the following:

3a. *A more radical challenge to existing doctrine?* In Ricci v. DeStefano, 129 S. Ct. 2658 (2009), Justice Scalia raised the possibility that strict scrutiny for racial classifications might raise doubts about the constitutionality of much of the edifice of modern antidiscrimination law. Recall that many federal antidiscrimination statutes — for example, Title VII of the Civil Rights Act of 1964, which deals with employment discrimination, and section 2 of the Voting Rights Act of 1965 — prohibit practices that have a disparate impact regardless of the defendant's intent. In *Ricci*, the Court faced a Title VII and equal protection clause-based challenge to a city's decision not to certify the results of a promotional test for firefighters in light of the test's disparate impact on black and Latino applicants. The Court disposed of the case on statutory grounds, not reaching the constitutional question. In his concurrence, however, Justice Scalia observed that the Court's decision

> merely postpones the evil day on which the Court will have to confront the question: Whether, or to what extent, are the disparate-impact provisions of Title VII of the Civil Rights Act of 1964 consistent with the Constitution's guarantee of equal protection? The question is not an easy one. See generally Primus, Equal Protection and Disparate Impact: Round Three, 117 Harv. L. Rev. 493 (2003).
>
> The difficulty is this: Whether or not Title VII's disparate-treatment provisions forbid "remedial" actions when a disparate-impact violation would

not otherwise result — the question resolved by the Court today — it is clear that Title VII not only permits but affirmatively *requires* such actions when a disparate-impact violation *would* otherwise result. But if the Federal Government is prohibited from discriminating on the basis of race, *Bolling v. Sharpe*, 347 U.S. 497, 500 (1954), then surely it is also prohibited from enacting laws mandating that third parties — *e.g.*, employers, whether private, State, or municipal — discriminate on the basis of race. See *Buchanan v. Warley,* 245 U.S. 60, 78-82 (1917)....

To be sure, the disparate-impact laws do not mandate imposition of quotas, but it is not clear why that should provide a safe harbor. Would a private employer not be guilty of unlawful discrimination if he refrained from establishing a racial hiring quota but intentionally designed his hiring practices to achieve the same end? Surely he would. Intentional discrimination is still occurring, just one step up the chain. Government compulsion of such design would therefore seemingly violate equal protection principles. Nor would it matter that Title VII requires consideration of race on a wholesale, rather than retail, level....

[T]he war between disparate impact and equal protection will be waged sooner or later, and it behooves us to begin thinking about how — and on what terms — to make peace between them.

E. Equal Protection Methodology: The Problem of Sexual Orientation

Page 678. At the beginning of section 3 of the Note, after the citation to Baehr v. Lewin, add the following:

Varnum v. Brien, 763 N.W.2d 862, (Iowa 2009);

Page 682. At the end of section 3 of the Note, add the following:

Following the California Supreme Court's decision in the Marriage Cases, the state's voters passed an initiative amending the state's constitution to provide that "Only marriage between a man and a woman is valid or recognized in California." In Strauss v. Horton, 46 Cal. 4th 364 (2009), the California

Supreme Court upheld the initiative against a state constitutional challenge, but observed that strict scrutiny remained the appropriate standard for assessing discrimination on the basis of sexual orientation under the California constitution. And it concluded that "although [the initiative] eliminates the ability of same-sex couples to enter into an official relationship designated 'marriage,' in all other respects those couples continue to possess, under the state constitutional privacy and due process clauses, 'the core set of basic *substantive* legal rights and attributes traditionally associated with marriage,' including, 'most fundamentally, the opportunity of an individual to establish — with the person with whom the individual has chosen to share his or her life — an *officially recognized and protected family* possessing mutual rights and responsibilities and entitled to the same respect and dignity accorded a union traditionally designated as marriage.'"

6 IMPLIED FUNDAMENTAL RIGHTS

A. *Introduction*

Page 713. Before section 4 of the Note, add the following:

For an argument that "deciding issues based on original meanings makes sense in some kinds of cases but not others," see Primus, When Should Original Meaning Matter?, 107 Mich. L. Rev. 165 (2008). With respect to arguments for originalism grounded in the Constitution's democratic origins, the author asserts that "[paying] attention to original meanings makes sense in cases construing provisions that were adopted recently enough that the dead-hand problem does not arise. Original meaning [gradually] becomes less important until the provision's democratic authority expires completely." Id. at 169. With respect to arguments for originalism grounded in the rule of law, the author asserts that the arguments "[make] sense only in cases where the provision's original meaning is also its operative meaning, where 'operative meaning' is the meaning that a provision has to its contemporary audience. [If] a contrary meaning has taken hold, [then] displacing that operative meaning in favor of the original meaning might undermine the very rule-of-law values that originalist reasoning is supposed to support." Id. at 170.

Page 715. Before section 5 of the Note, add the following:

For a skeptical analysis of public-meaning originalism in the context of *Heller*, see Tushnet, *Heller* and the New Originalism, 69 Ohio St. L.J. 609 (2008). The author concludes that "[unfortunately], the new originalism cannot deliver on its promises, as *Heller* shows. The reason is simple: The new originalism's search for *the*—that is, the single—conventional understanding of constitutional terms is doomed, at least in the most interesting cases. [History] is replete with ['contested] truths.' These contests are precisely contests over conventional meaning."

G. *Procedural Due Process*

Page 951. At the end of section 1c of the Note, add the following:

d. *DNA testing.* In District Attorney's Office for the Third Judicial District v. Osborne, 129 S. Ct. 2308 (2009), the Court, in a five-to-four decision written by Chief Justice Roberts, held that there was no liberty interest in access to DNA evidence. Osborne had been convicted sixteen years earlier of kidnapping, assault, and sexual assault. The evidence against him included a statement by Jackson, who admitted to participating in the rape and assault, that Osborne had been a passenger in his car during the incident; an uncertain photo identification by the victim; statements by other witnesses that shortly before the incident, Jackson had driven off with Osborne; and an axe handle, similar to the one at the scene of the crime, found in Osborne's room.

The state performed DQ Alpha DNA testing on sperm found in a condom left at the scene. This is a relatively inexact form of DNA testing. The semen had a genotype that matched a blood sample taken from Osborne. Osborne is black, and approximately 16 percent of black individuals have this genotype.

Osborne's trial lawyer later testified that she did not request RFLP testing, a more precise DNA procedure, because she believed her client guilty and thought that the more precise test would harm his defense. However, Osborne claimed that he had specifically asked his lawyer to request the more precise test. The lawyer stated that she had no memory of Osborne making this request, but said that she was "willing to accept" that he had.

After his conviction, Osborne admitted his guilt in the course of parole hearings—a requirement in order to be eligible for parole.

In this federal lawsuit, Osborne claimed the right to access to the DNA evidence so that he could perform at his own expense STR testing—a much more accurate DNA procedure that was not available at the time of his trial.

Writing for the Court, Chief Justice Roberts observed that "the availability of technologies not available at trial cannot mean that every criminal conviction or even every criminal conviction involving biological evidence, is suddenly in doubt. The dilemma is how to harness DNA's power to prove innocence without unnecessarily overthrowing the established system of criminal justice. [That] task belongs primarily to the legislature."

Chief Justice Roberts observed that forty-six states, although not Alaska, where this case arose, had enacted statutes dealing with access to DNA. These laws, while allowing some access, also imposed conditions like a requirement of demonstrating materiality or a sworn statement that the applicant is innocent.

The Court acknowledged that Osborne had a liberty interest in demonstrating his innocence with new evidence under state law. It did not follow, however that "the Due Process Clause requires that certain familiar preconviction trial rights be extended to protect Osborne's postconviction liberty interest. [A] criminal defendant proved guilty after a fair trial does not have the same liberty interests as a free man."

According to the Court, the standard was "whether consideration of Osborne's claim within the framework of the State's procedures for postconviction relief 'offends some principle of justice so rooted in the traditions and conscience of our people as to be ranked as fundamental,' or 'transgresses any recognized principle of fundamental fairness in operation.'" (Quoting Medina v. California, 505 U.S. 437, 446, 448 (1992)).

The Court found Alaska's procedures adequate under this standard.

> Alaska provides a substantive right to be released on a sufficiently compelling showing of new evidence that establishes innocence. [The] State provides for discovery in postconviction proceedings, and has [specified] that this discovery procedure is available to those seeking access to DNA evidence. These procedures are not without limits. The evidence must indeed be newly available, [must] have been diligently pursued, and must also be sufficiently material. These procedures [are] not inconsistent with the "traditions and conscience of our people" or with "any recognized principle of fundamental fairness."

The Court also rejected Osborne's claim that he had been denied substantive due process, a claim that it characterized as "a freestanding right to DNA evidence untethered from the liberty interests he hopes to vindicate with it."

> The elected governments of the States are actively confronting the challenges DNA technology poses to our criminal justice systems and our traditional notions of finality, as well as the opportunities it affords. To suddenly constitutionalize this area would short-circuit what looks to be a prompt and considered legislative response.

In a concurring opinion, Justice Alito, joined by Justice Kennedy and joined in this part by Justice Thomas, pointed out that the state had valid interests in denying DNA testing. DNA testing "often fails to provide 'absolute proof' of anything." Moreover, "the State has important interests in maintaining the integrity of its evidence, and the risks associated with evidence contamination increase every time someone attempts to extract new DNA from a sample." Finally, Justice Alito noted that "[the] resources required to process and analyze [hundreds] of thousands of samples have created severe backlogs in state crime labs across the country."

Justice Stevens, joined by Justices Ginsburg and Breyer and joined in part by Justice Souter, dissented:

> The State of Alaska possesses physical evidence that, if tested, will conclusively establish whether [Osborne] committed rape and attempted murder. If he did, justice has been served by his conviction and sentence. If not, Osborne has needlessly spent decades behind bars while the true culprit has not been brought to justice. The DNA test Osborne seeks is a simple one, its cost modest, and its results uniquely precise. Yet for reasons the State has been unable or unwilling to articulate, it refuses to allow Osborne to test the evidence at his own expense and to thereby ascertain the truth once and for all.

Contrary to the majority's position, Justice Stevens argued that state procedures were inadequate to provide Osborne with access to the evidence and that "[t]he fact that nearly all the States have now recognized some post-conviction right to DNA evidence makes it more, not less, appropriate to recognize a limited federal right to such evidence in cases where litigants are unfairly barred from obtaining relief in state court."

Justice Souter also filed a dissenting opinion.

Page 960. After section 4 of the Note, add the following:

5. *Bias.* Does the Due Process Clause guarantee an unbiased decisionmaker? What does "bias" mean in this context?

Consider Caperton v. A. T. Massey Coal Co., 129 S. Ct. 2252 (2009). A West Virginia jury found that defendant Massey was guilty of fraudulent misrepresentation, concealment, and tortuous interference with existing contractual relations and awarded plaintiff Caperton $50 million in damages. Knowing that the Supreme Court of Appeals of West Virginia would consider an appeal in the case, Blankenship, Massey's chairman and chief executive officer, spent over $3 million directly and indirectly supporting the election of Benjamin to a seat on the Court. This was more than the total amount spent by all other Benjamin supporters, three times the amount spent by Benjamin's own committee, and apparently, $1 million more than the total amount spent by the campaign committees of both candidates combined. Benjamin won the election. Despite repeated requests that he recuse himself, Benjamin sat on the appeal in the Massey case and cast the deciding vote in a three-to-two decision to reverse the result below.

In a five-to-four decision, the Court, in an opinion by Justice Kennedy, held that the due process clause required Benjamin's recusal. The Court noted that "[n]ot every campaign contribution by a litigant or attorney creates a probability of bias that requires a judge's recusal, but this is an exceptional case."

> [There] is a serious risk of actual bias — based on objective and reasonable perceptions — when a person with a personal stake in a particular case had a significant and disproportionate influence in placing the judge on the case by raising funds or directing the judge's election campaign when the case was pending or imminent. The inquiry centers on the contribution's relative size in comparison to the total amount of money contributed to the campaign, the total amount spent in the election, and the apparent effect such contribution had on the outcome of the election. . . .
>
> Just as no man is allowed to be a judge in his own cause, similar fears of bias can arise when — without the consent of the other parties — a man chooses the judge in his own cause. And applying this principle to the judicial election process, there was here a serious, objective risk of actual bias that required Justice Benjamin's recusal.

Chief Justice Roberts, joined by Justices Scalia, Thomas, and Alito, dissented:

> I, of course, share the majority's sincere concerns about the need to maintain a fair, independent, and impartial judiciary — and one that appears to be such. But I fear that the Court's decision will undermine rather than promote these values. . . .
>
> Unlike the established grounds for disqualification, a "probability of bias" cannot be defined in any limited way. The Court's new "rule" provides no guidance to judges and litigants about when recusal will be

constitutionally required. This will inevitably lead to an increase in allegations that judges are biased, however groundless those charges may be. The end result will do far more to erode public confidence in judicial impartiality than an isolated failure to recuse in a particular case.

Justice Scalia also wrote a dissenting opinion.

7
FREEDOM OF EXPRESSION

B. *Content-Based Restrictions: Dangerous Ideas and Information*

Page 1042. After section 5 of the Note, add the following:

5A. *Why should it matter whether the harm is imminent?* Consider Healy, Brandenburg in a Time of Terror, 84 Notre Dame L. Rev. 655, 705-709 (2009):

> When a speaker urges listeners to commit a crime right now or very soon and those listeners are likely to comply, there is almost nothing the government or anyone else can do to prevent the crime from occurring. [The] government's only alternative is to criminalize the advocacy in the hope of deterring speakers from engaging in it to begin with. But when a speaker urges listeners to violate law in the future, the government has several alternatives. First, [the] police have at least some ability to prevent the crime from occurring. [Second], when a speaker advocates future crime, other speakers have an opportunity to rebut his arguments and discourage his listeners from breaking the law. [The] third alternative to government regulation is not so much an alternative as a reason to think that prohibiting advocacy of future crime is not necessary to prevent the crime from occurring. When a speaker urges listeners to break the law, they may initially be persuaded by the force of his arguments and the intensity of his convictions. But as time passes and listeners reflect on the speaker's message, the persuasive force of his words may diminish. This seems especially likely when listeners are urged to violate the [law, because most] people are socially conditioned to follow the law and do not commit crimes lightly. [Finally], determining whether criminal advocacy is likely to lead to crime is not easy.

> The success of speech depends on a range of factors that cannot easily be assessed by the speaker at the time he speaks, by the police at the time of arrest, or by courts at the time of trial. In addition, because those who advocate crime are usually not sympathetic, the likelihood of success is almost certain to be overestimated.

Page 1066. After section 4 of the Note, add the following:

4A. *A Comparative Perspective.* Mehdi Zana is the former mayor of Diyarbakur, the largest city in southeast Turkey. In 1985, serious disturbances erupted in this area of Turkey between the government's security forces and members of the PKK (Workers' Party of Kurdistan). The PKK's aim was to bring about the secession of part of Turkey's territory, and to achieve that end it committed widespread acts of violence, including murder, kidnapping, and armed robbery. By 1996, the confrontation had claimed the lives of 4,036 civilians and 3,884 members of the security forces. During this time, ten of the eleven provinces in southeast Turkey had been subjected to emergency rule. In this context, Zana made the following remarks in an interview with journalists: "I support the PKK, [but] I am not in favour of massacres. Anyone can make mistakes, and the PKK kill women and children by mistake." This statement was widely circulated in the media. Zana was prosecuted under Turkish law for having "defended an act punishable by law as a serious crime" and "endangering public safety." What result under *Brandenburg*? Is that the "right" result?

Zana was convicted by the Turkish National Security Court and he appealed to the European Court of Human Rights, arguing that his conviction violated Article 10 of the Convention for the Protection of Human Rights and Fundamental Freedoms, which provides:

> Everyone has the right to freedom of expression. This right shall include freedom to hold opinions and to receive and impart information and ideas without interference by public authority. [The] exercise of these freedoms, since it carries with it duties and responsibilities, may be subject to such formalities, conditions, restrictions or penalties as are prescribed by law and are necessary in a democratic society, in the interests of national security, territorial integrity or public safety, for the prevention of disorder or crime, for the protection of health or morals, for the protection of the reputation or rights of others, for preventing the disclosure of information received in confidence, or for maintaining the authority and impartiality of the judiciary.

In Zana v. Turkey, 27 Eur. H.R. Rep. 667 (1997), excerpted in Gey, Free Speech and the Incitement of Violence or Unlawful Behavior: Statutes Directed at Speech, in V. Amar & M. Tushnet, Global Perspectives on Constitutional Law 146 (2009), the court stated:

> [Zana's] words could be interpreted in several ways but, at all events, they are both contradictory and ambiguous. [The] statement cannot, however, be looked at in isolation. It had a specific significance in the circumstances of the cases, as [Zana] must have realized. [In] those circumstances the support given to the PKK [by] the former mayor of [the] most important city in south-east Turkey, in an interview published in a major national daily newspaper, had to be regarded as likely to exacerbate an already explosive situation. [Having regard to all these factors, [the] Court considers that the interference [with freedom of speech] was proportionate to the legitimate aims pursued. There has consequently been no breach of Article 10 of the Convention.

For a similar analysis, consider President Lincoln's approach to free speech in a strikingly similar situation during the Civil War. See G. Stone, Perilous Times: Free Speech in Wartime 94-120 (2004).

Page 1067. At the end of section 1 of the Note, add the following:

More broadly, to what extent does the First Amendment protect a right of "intellectual privacy"—that is, a right that limits the authority of the government to gather information about our phone calls, email communications, reading habits, and Internet usage? Consider Richards, Intellectual Privacy, 87 Tex. L. Rev. 387, 394, 399, 403-404 (2008):

> [T]he processes protected by intellectual privacy occur before we are ready to speak. These protections are not so much right to speak as they are the ways in which our minds develop something novel or interesting to say. [The] threat to intellectual privacy has [become particularly] significant in recent years with the growth of new technologies and the creation of massive quantities of intellectual records. [Imagine] a system of free speech that is deeply protective of the act of speaking, but which has little protection for the act of thinking. Under a system like this, people could speak freely on a whole host of controversial issues [but] the government would be free to secretly monitor phone calls, Internet usage, and the movements and asso-

ciations of individuals. [If] we value [the] cognitive processes that produce new ideas, then some measure of intellectual privacy, some respite from cognitive surveillance, is essential.

D. Content-Based Restrictions: "Low" Value Speech

Page 1175. At the end of section 1 of the Note, add the following:

Bezanson, Art and the Constitution 93 Iowa L. Rev. 1593 (2008).

Page 1214. Before section 1 of the Note, add the following:

1A. *Fleeting expletives and the continuing viability of* Pacifica. In 2004, the Federal Communications Commission amended the approach that was upheld in *Pacifica* and held for the first time that any use of the words "fuck" and "shit" could be actionably indecent, even if the word was not used in a sexual manner and even if it was used only once. The 2004 order dealt with an NBC broadcast of the Golden Globe Awards, in which the singer Bono commented, "This is really, really fucking brilliant." The Commission explained that the broadcast was "patently offensive" because the word "fuck" "is one of the most vulgar, graphic and explicit descriptions of sexual activity in the English language." The Commission argued that its action was necessary to "safeguard the well-being of the nation's children from the most objectionable, most offensive language."

FCC v. Fox Television Stations, 129 S. Ct. 1800 (2009), dealt with decisions by the FCC involving the singer Cher's use of the word "fuck" during the Billboard Music Awards ("I've also had critics for the last forty years saying that I was on my way out every year. Right. So fuck 'em.") and the actress Nicole Richie's use of the words "shit" and "fucking" in another award ceremony ("Have you ever tried to get cow shit out of a Prada purse? It's not so fucking simple."). In both instances, the FCC held that the fleeting use of these expletives violated its new 2004 order. The Court of Appeals held that the 2004 order was invalid under the Administrative Procedure Act because it was arbitrary and capricious. The Supreme Court reversed, but did not reach the First Amendment question.

In his opinion for the Court, Justice Scalia offered the following observation that is relevant to the continuing vitality of *Pacifica*: "[The Court of Appeals] believed that children today 'likely hear this language far more often from other sources than they did in the 1970's when the Commission first began sanctioning indecent speech,' and that cuts against more stringent regulation of broadcasts. Assuming the premise is true, [the] conclusion does not necessarily follow. The Commission could reasonably conclude that the pervasiveness of foul language, and the coarsening of public entertainment in other media such as cable, justify more stringent regulation of broadcast programs so as to give conscientious parents a relatively safe haven for their children."

In a concurring opinion, Justice Thomas called *Pacifica* into question. Noting that *Pacifica* was premised in part on the doctrine that the government could regulate broadcasting more than other means of communication because of the "scarcity of broadcast frequencies," Thomas argued that that doctrine was incoherent in 1978 and, in any event, had completely been outstripped by technological advances in the years since.

Justice Breyer, joined by Justices Stevens, Souter, and Ginsburg, dissented on the ground that the 2004 order violated the Administrative Procedure Act.

E. Content-Neutral Restrictions

Page 1273. At the end of section 9 of the Note, add the following:

Wells, Privacy and Funeral Protests, 87 N.C. L. Rev. 151 (2008).

Page 1274. At the end of section 10 of the Note, add the following:

See also Krotoszynski, The Return of Seditious Libel, 55 UCLA L. Rev. 1239 (2008) (criticizing federal courts for upholding such restrictions by crediting inflated claims of security needs when the real motive for the restrictions is the desire of political leaders not to be embarrassed by speech that criticizes them).

Page 1291. At the end of section 2 of the Note, add the following:

Suppose a town has an ordinance prohibiting any use of a loudspeaker in a residential neighborhood between the hours of 8:00 P.M. and 8:00 A.M. Presumably, this ordinance is a constitutional, content-neutral regulation of speech. Now suppose the town amends the ordinance to allow the use of loudspeakers in residential neighborhoods until 10:00 P.M. for political campaign speech within two weeks of an election. Is the amended ordinance unconstitutional after *Mosley*? Consider Ammori, Beyond Content-Neutrality: Understanding Content-Based Promotion of Democratic Speech, 61 Fed. Comm. L. J. 273, 277, 283, 324 (2009):

> Government need not be "neutral" regarding speech [that] is traditionally believed necessary for an informed citizenry. [Free] speech doctrine [should] explicitly distinguish between laws meant to promote [content] necessary for an informed citizenry and those meant to suppress disfavored content. [Content-promoting] laws do not necessarily reflect a censorial purpose. [Laws] promoting democratic content pose different risks from content-based laws meant to suppress disfavored content, and the constitutional test applied to content-promoting laws should focus on the main risk: viewpoint discrimination.

Page 1299. After section 1 of the Note, add the following:

1A. *Payroll deductions for political activities.* Until 2003, public employees in Idaho could authorize both a payroll deduction for general union dues and a separate payroll deduction for union political activities. In 2003, the Idaho legislature prohibited payroll deductions for political purposes. A group of Idaho public employee unions challenged the 2003 legislation on the ground that it violated the First Amendment. In Ysursa v. Pocatello Education Association, 129 S. Ct. 1093 (2009), the Court rejected this claim.

Chief Justice Roberts wrote the opinion of the Court: "Restrictions on speech based on its content are 'presumptively invalid' and subject to strict scrutiny. [But 'a] legislature's decision not to subsidize the exercise of a fundamental right does not infringe the right, and thus is not subject to strict scrutiny.' [The] State is not constitutionally obligated to provide payroll deductions at all. [While] publicly administered payroll deductions for political purposes can enhance the unions' exercise of First Amendment rights, Idaho is under no obligation to aid the unions in their political activities. And the State's decision not to do so is not an abridgment of the unions' speech. [Given] that the State has not infringed the unions' First Amendment rights, the State need only demonstrate a rational basis to justify the ban on political payroll deductions. [The] prohibition is [justified] by the State's interest in avoiding the reality or appearance of government favoritism or entanglement with partisan politics."

Justice Ginsburg filed a concurring opinion. Justices Stevens, Breyer, and Souter filed dissenting opinions. Would the outcome be different if the State prohibited payroll deductions to support the Democratic Party? Would the outcome be different if the State prohibited private employers from allowing payroll deductions for political purposes? In fact, the 2003 legislation prohibited private employers from allowing such deductions. The State conceded that that part of the 2003 statute violated the First Amendment. Why should it matter whether the law restricts private employers rather than public employers?

Page 1313. At the end of section 3 of the Note, add the following:

Consider also Norton, The Measure of Government Speech: Identifying Expression's Source, 88 B.U.L. Rev. 587, 589, 595-597, 629-630 (2008):

> [T]he Supreme Court has shielded the government's expression from Free Speech Clause scrutiny. [Government] speech merits this insulation because it is both inevitable and valuable. In particular, government speech facilitates significant First Amendment interests in sharing knowledge and discovering truth by informing the public on a wide range of topics. [A] message's source can have positive or negative effects on its persuasiveness, depending on observers' assessments of the source's credibility [and] because public attitudes towards government vary widely [assessments] of government credibility differ too. [One danger of government speech is] that the government may manipulate the public's attitudes towards its views by deliberately obscuring its identity as a message's source. Government speech is thus most valuable and least dangerous when its government source is apparent, enabling the public to more accurately assess the message's credibility. . . .
>
> In *Rust*, [doctors and nurses] delivered the contested counseling [without] any requirement that its governmental origins be disclosed. Under these circumstances, patients might well misunderstand clinic employees to be offering their own independent counsel, rather than speaking as agents required to espouse the government's view. [Because] health professionals may be seen as more credible than the government in this setting based on

public perception of their expertise and objectivity, patients may have been misled into evaluating the counseling differently than they would have if the speakers had made clear its governmental source. [*Rust*] thus illustrates the danger of treating expression that fails to satisfy the demands of functional transparency as government speech free from First Amendment scrutiny.

Page 1317. Before *National Endowment for the Arts v. Finley*, add the following:

PLEASANT GROVE CITY, UTAH V. SUMMUM, 129 S. CT. 1129 (2009). Pioneer Park, a public park in Pleasant Grove City, contains fifteen permanent displays, eleven of which were donated to the city by private groups. These include an historic granary, a wishing well, a September 11 monument, and a Ten Commandments monument donated by the Fraternal Order of Eagles in 1971. Summum is a religious organization founded in 1975 and headquartered in Salt Lake City. In 2003, Summum's president requested permission to erect a stone monument in Pioneer Park. The monument would contain the Seven Aphorisms of Summum, which according to Summum doctrine were inscribed on the original tablet handed down by God to Moses on Mount Sinai. The city denied the request, explaining that it permitted monuments to be displayed in the park only if they "directly related to the history of Pleasant Grove" or they "were donated by groups with longstanding ties to the Pleasant Grove community." The Court of Appeals for the Tenth Circuit held that because public parks have traditionally been regarded as public forums, the city could not constitutionally reject the Seven Aphorisms monument absent a compelling justification for doing so. In a unanimous decision, the Supreme Court reversed.

Justice Alito delivered the opinion of the Court: "The [fundamental] disagreement [centers] on the nature of [the city's] conduct when [it] permitted privately donated monuments to be erected in Pioneer Park. [Was the city] engaging in [its] own expressive conduct? Or [was it] providing a forum for private speech? [If the city was] engaging in [its] own expressive conduct, then the Free Speech Clause has no application. The Free Speech Clause restricts government regulation of private speech; it does not regulate government speech. [Citing *Rust*.] [Indeed,] it is not easy to imagine how government could function if it lacked this freedom. . . .

"While government speech is not restricted by the Free Speech Clause, the government does not have a free hand to regulate private speech on government property. [There] may be situations in which it is difficult to tell whether a government entity is speaking on its own behalf or is providing a forum for private speech, but this case does not present such a situation. Permanent monuments displayed on public property typically represent government speech. [When] a government entity arranges for the construction of a monument, it does so because it wishes to convey some thought or instill some feeling in those who see the structure. [Just] as government-commissioned and government-financed monuments speak for the government, so do privately financed and donated monuments that the government accepts and displays to the public on government land. [Throughout] our Nation's history, the general government practice with respect to donated monuments has been one of selective receptivity. [Government] decisionmakers select the monuments that portray what they view as appropriate for the place in question, taking into account such content-based factors as esthetics, history, and local culture. The monuments that are accepted, therefore, are meant to convey and have the effect of conveying a government message, and they thus constitute government speech. . . .

"[Summum] voices the legitimate concern that the government speech doctrine not be used as a subterfuge for favoring certain private speakers over others based on viewpoint. [Summum] and the Court of Appeals analogize the installation of permanent monuments in a public park to the delivery of speeches and the holding of marches and demonstrations, and they thus invoke the rule that a public park is a traditional public forum for these activities. But 'public forum principles . . . are out of place in the context of this case.' The forum doctrine has been applied in situations in which government-owned property or a government program was capable of accommodating a large number of public speakers without defeating the essential function of the land or the program. For example, a park can accommodate many speakers and, over time, many parades and demonstrations. [A] public university's student activity fund can provide money for many campus activities. [Citing *Rosenberger*.] A public university's buildings may offer meeting space for hundreds of student groups. [Citing *Widmar*.] [By] contrast, public parks can accommodate only a limited number of permanent monuments. [It] is hard to imagine how a public park could be opened up for the installation of permanent monuments by every person or group wishing to engage in that form of expression. [Indeed,] if public parks were considered to be traditional public forums for the purpose of erecting privately donated monuments, most parks would have little choice but to refuse all such donations. And where the application of forum analysis would lead almost inexorably to closing of the forum, it is obvious that forum analysis is out of place. [Therefore,] forum analysis simply does not apply to the installation of permanent monuments on public property.

"[We] hold that the City's decision to accept certain privately donated monuments while rejecting [Summum's] is best viewed as a form of government speech. As a result, the City's decision is not subject to the Free Speech Clause. . . . "

Justice Stevens, joined by Justice Ginsburg, filed a concurring opinion, noting that the Court's "recently minted government speech doctrine" is "of doubtful merit." Justice Scalia, joined by Justice Thomas, filed concurring opinion, emphasizing that the city's display of the Ten Commandments monument does not violate the Establishment Clause. Justice Breyer filed a concurring opinion, arguing that the government speech doctrine must be understood as "a rule of thumb, not a rigid category." Justice Souter filed a concurring opinion, expressing "qualms" about the argument that "public monuments are government speech categorically."

How does one square this decision with the establishment clause? Can the city, invoking the government speech doctrine, legitimately allow a twenty-foot-high cross to be displayed in a public park as an exercise of government speech? See the discussion of the *McCreary County* and *Van Orden* cases at page 1487 of the main text.

Page 1325. At the end of the page, add the following:

For the view that the Framers understood the First Amendment to protect symbolic expression, see Volokh, Symbolic Expression and the Original Meaning of the First Amendment, 97 Geo. L.J. 1057 (2009).

Page 1357. After section 2e of the Note, add the following:

3. *A comparative perspective.* The Canada Elections Act of 2000 set limits for third party spending in elections. Specifically, the Act provides that a third-party (that is, a group or individual who is not a candidate) "shall not incur election advertising expenses of a total amount of more than $150,000 during an election period in relation to a general election" and "not more than $3,000 [to] promote or oppose the election of one or more candidates in a given electoral district." The act defines "election advertising expenses" as including any paid message that names candidates, shows their likeness, or takes a position on an issue "with which they are particularly associated." Stephen Harper, the head of a conservative political group, brought suit claiming that the act violated the Canadian Charter of Rights and Freedoms, which guarantees to every person the fundamental "freedom of thought, belief, opinion and expression." The Charter provides that fundamental freedoms may be subjected "only to such reasonable limits [as] can be demonstrably justified in a free and democratic society." In Harper v. Canada, 1 S.C.R. 827 (2004), excerpted in Hasen, Regulation of

Campaign Finance, in V. Amar and M. Tushnet, Global Perspectives on Constitutional Law 198 (2009), the Supreme Court of Canada upheld these provisions of the act, therefore reaching a different result than the Supreme Court of the United States in *Buckley*.

Justice Bastarache delivered the opinion of the court: "Third party advertising is political expression. [As such, it] lies at the core of the expression guaranteed by the Charter and warrants a high degree of constitutional protection. [In] some circumstances, however, third party advertising will be less deserving of constitutional protection. Indeed, it is possible that third parties have access to significant financial resources can manipulate political discourse to their advantage through political advertising. [Advertising] expense limits may restrict free expression to ensure that participants are able to meaningfully participate in the electoral process. For candidates, political parties and third parties, meaningful participation means the ability to inform voters of their position. For voters, meaningful participation means the ability to hear and weigh many points of view. The difficulties of striking this balance are evident. . . .

"The question, then, is what promotes an informed voter? For voters to be able to hear all points of view, the information disseminated by third parties, candidates, and political parties cannot be unlimited. In the absence of spending limits, it is possible for the affluent or a number of persons or groups pooling their resources and acting in concert to dominate the political discourse. [If] a few groups are able to flood the electoral discourse with their message, it is possible, indeed likely, that the voices of some will be drowned out. Where those having access to the most resources monopolize the election discourse, their opponents will be deprived of a reasonable opportunity to speak and be heard. This unequal dissemination of points of view undermines the voter's ability to be adequately informed of all views. In this way, equality in the political discourse is necessary for meaningfully participation in the electoral process and ultimately enhances the right to vote."

F. Freedom of the Press

Page 1406. At the end of section 2 of the Note, add the following:

For data on the number of subpoenas served on the press in recent years, see Jones, Avalanche or Undue Alarm? An Empirical Study of Subpoenas Received by the New Media, 93 Minn. L. Rev. 585 (2008).

Page 1426. After section 2c of the Note, add the following:

cc. In FCC v. Fox Television Stations, 129 S. Ct. 1800 (2009), discussed *supra* in the Supplement to page 1274, Justice Thomas called *Red Lion* into question in a separate concurring opinion:

> *Red Lion* [was] unconvincing when [it was] issued, and the passage of time has only increased doubt regarding [its] continued validity. [*Red Lion*] relied heavily on the scarcity of available broadcast frequencies. [Its] deep intrusion into the First Amendment rights of broadcasters [is] problematic on two levels. First, instead of looking to first principles to evaluate the constitutional question, the Court relied on a set of transitory facts [to] determine the applicable First Amendment standard. But the original meaning of the Constitution cannot turn on modern necessity. [Highlighting] the doctrinal incoherence of *Red Lion*, [the] Court has declined to apply the lesser standard of First Amendment scrutiny imposed on broadcast speech to federal regulation of telephone dial-in services [citing *Sable Communications*], cable television programming [citing *Turner Broadcasting*], and the Internet [citing Reno v. American Civil Liberties Union]. The justifications relied on by the Court in *Red Lion* [neither] distinguish broadcast from cable, nor explain the relaxed application of the principles of the First Amendment to broadcast. . . .
>
> Second, even if this Court's disfavored treatment of broadcasters under the First Amendment could have been justified at the time of *Red Lion*, dramatic technological advances have eviscerated the factual assumptions underlying [that decision]. Broadcast spectrum is significantly less scarce than it was 40 years ago. [And] the trend should continue. [Moreover], traditional broadcast television and radio are no longer the 'uniquely pervasive' media forms they once were. For most consumers, traditional broadcast media programming is now bundled with cable or satellite services. Broadcast and other video programming is also widely available over the Internet. [The] extant facts that drove this Court to subject broadcasters to unique disfavor under the First Amendment simply do not exist today.

8
THE CONSTITUTION AND RELIGION

B. The Establishment Clause

Page 1488. At the end of section 3 of the Note, add the following:

See also Pleasant Grove City, Utah v. Summum, 129 S. Ct. 1129 (2009), discussed *supra* in the Supplement to page 1317.

D. Permissible Accommodation

Page 1537. At the end of the first paragraph, add the following:

For a related view, see Gellman & Looper-Friedman, Thou Shalt Use the Equal Protection Clause for Religion Cases (Not Just the Establishment Clause), 10 U. Pa. J. Const'l L. 666 (2008).